The Collected Works of
Effie Waller Smith

THE SCHOMBURG LIBRARY OF
NINETEENTH-CENTURY BLACK WOMEN WRITERS

Henry Louis Gates, Jr.
General Editor

Titles are listed chronologically; collections that
include works published over a span of years are listed according to
the publication date of their initial work.

The Collected Works
of
Effie Waller Smith

With an Introduction by
DAVID DESKINS

New York   Oxford
OXFORD UNIVERSITY PRESS
1991

PS
3537
M36
1991

Oxford University Press

Oxford   New York   Toronto
Delhi   Bombay   Calcutta   Madras   Karachi
Petaling Jaya   Singapore   Hong Kong   Tokyo
Nairobi   Dar es Salaam   Cape Town
Melbourne   Auckland

and associated companies in
Berlin   Ibadan

Library of Congress Cataloging-in-Publication Data
Smith, Effie Waller, 1879–1960.
[Works. 1991]
The collected works of Effie Waller Smith /
with an introduction by David Deskins.
p.   cm.—(The Schomburg library of nineteenth-century Black women writers)
Includes bibliographical references.
ISBN 0-19-506197-7
I. Title.   II. Series.
PS3537.M36   1991
811'.52—dc20   90-38942   CIP

2 4 6 8 10 9 7 5 3 1

Printed in the United States of America
on acid free paper

The
Schomburg Library
of
Nineteenth-Century
Black Women Writers
Is
Dedicated
in Memory
of
PAULINE AUGUSTA COLEMAN GATES

1916–1987

PUBLISHER'S NOTE

Whenever possible, the volumes in this set were reproduced directly from original materials. When availability, physical condition of original texts, or other circumstances prohibited this, volumes or portions of volumes were reset.

FOREWORD TO THE
SCHOMBURG SUPPLEMENT

Henry Louis Gates, Jr.

The enthusiastic reception by students, scholars, and the general public to the 1988 publication of the Schomburg Library of Nineteenth-Century Black Women Writers more than justified the efforts of twenty-five scholars and the staff of the Black Periodical Literature Project to piece together the fragments of knowledge about the writings of African-American women between 1773 and 1910. The Library's republication of those writings in thirty volumes—ranging from the poetry of Phillis Wheatley to the enormous body of work that emerged out of the "Black Woman's Era" at the turn of this century—was a *beginning* for the restoration of the written sensibilities of a group of writers who confronted the twin barriers of racism and sexism in America. Through their poetry, diaries, speeches, biographies, essays, fictional narratives, and autobiographies, these writers transcended the boundaries of racial prejudice and sexual discrimination by recording the thoughts and feelings of Americans who were, at once, black *and* female. Taken together, these works configure into a literary tradition because their authors read, critiqued, and revised each other's words, in textual groundings with their sisters.

Indeed, by publishing these texts together as a "library," and by presenting them as part of a larger discourse on race and gender, we hoped to enable readers to chart the formal specificities of this tradition and to trace its origins. As a whole, the works in the Schomburg Library demonstrate that the contemporary literary movement of African-American women writers is heir to a legacy that was born in 1773, when Phillis Wheatley's *Poems on Various Subjects, Religious and Moral* first unveiled the mind of a black woman to the world. The fact that the Wheatley volume has proven to be the most popular in the Schomburg set is a testament to her role as the "founder" of both the black American's and the black woman's literary tradition.

Even before the Library was published, however, I began to receive queries about producing a supplement that would incorporate works that had not been included initially. Often these exchanges were quite dramatic. For instance, shortly before a lecture I was about to deliver at the University of Cincinnati, Professor Sharon Dean asked me if the Library would be reprinting the 1859 autobiography of Eliza Potter, a black hairdresser who had lived and worked in Cincinnati. I had never heard of Potter, I replied. Did Dean have a copy of her book? No, but there *was* a copy at the Cincinnati Historical Society. As I delivered my lecture, I could not help thinking about this "lost" text and its great significance. In fact, after the lecture, Dean and I rushed from the building and drove to the Historical Society, arriving just a few moments before closing time. A patient librarian brought us the book, and as I leafed through it, I was once again confronted with the realization that so often accompanied the research behind the Library's first thirty volumes—the exciting, yet poignant awareness that there probably exist *dozens* of works like Potter's, buried in research libraries, waiting only to be uncovered through an accident of contiguity like that which placed Sharon Dean in Cincinnati, roaming the shelves of its Historical Society. Another scholar wrote to me about work being done on the poet Effie Waller Smith. Several other scholars also wrote to share their research on other authors and their works. A supplement to the Library clearly was necessary.

Thus we have now added ten volumes, among them Potter's autobiography and Smith's collected poetry, as well as a narrative by Sojourner Truth, several pamphlets by Ida B. Wells-Barnett, and two biographies by Josephine Brown and Frances Rollin. Also included are books consisting of various essays, stories, poems, and plays whose authors did not, or could not, collect their writings into a full-length volume. The works of Olivia Ward Bush-Banks, Angelina Weld Grimké, and Katherine Davis Chapman Tillman are in this category. A related volume is an anthology of short fiction published by black women in the *Colored American Magazine* and *Crisis* magazine—a collection that reveals the shaping influence which certain periodicals had upon the generation of specific genres within the black women's literary tradition. Both types of collected books are intended to kindle an interest in still another series of works that bring together for the first time either the complete *oeuvre* of one writer or that of one genre within the periodical press. Indeed, there are several authors whose collected works will establish them as major forces in the nineteenth- and early twentieth-century black women's intellectual community. Compiling, editing, and publishing these volumes will be as important a factor in constructing the black women's literary tradition as has been the republication of books long out of print.

Finally, the Library now includes a detailed bibliography of the writings of black women in the nineteenth and early twentieth centuries. Prepared by Jean Fagan Yellin and Cynthia Bond, this bibliography is the result of years of research and will serve as an indispensable resource in future investigations of black women writers, particularly those whose works appeared frequently throughout the nineteenth century in the principal conduit of writing for black women *or* men, the African-American periodical press.

The publication of this ten-volume supplement, we hope, will make a sound contribution toward reestablishing the importance of the creative works of African-American women and reevaluating the relation of these works not only to each other but also to African-American *and* American literature and history as a whole. These works are invaluable sources for readers intent upon understanding the complex interplay of ethnicity and gender, of racism and sexism—of how "race" becomes gendered and how gender becomes racialized—in American society.

FOREWORD
In Her Own Write

⟶ Henry Louis Gates, Jr. ⟵

One muffled strain in the Silent South, a jarring chord and a vague and uncomprehended cadenza has been and still is the Negro. And of that muffled chord, the one mute and voiceless note has been the sadly expectant Black Women, ...

The "other side" has not been represented by one who "lives there." And not many can more sensibly realize and more accurately tell the weight and the fret of the "long dull pain" than the open-eyed but hitherto voiceless Black Woman of America.

. . . as our Caucasian barristers are not to blame if they cannot *quite* put themselves in the dark man's place, neither should the dark man be wholly expected fully and adequately to reproduce the exact Voice of the Black Woman.

—Anna Julia Cooper
A Voice From the South (1892)

The birth of the African-American literary tradition occurred in 1773, when Phillis Wheatley published a book of poetry. Despite the fact that her book garnered for her a remarkable amount of attention, Wheatley's journey to the printer had been a most arduous one. Sometime in 1772, a young African girl walked demurely into a room in Boston to undergo an oral examination, the results of which would determine the direction of her life and work. Perhaps she was shocked

upon entering the appointed room. For there, perhaps gathered in a semicircle, sat eighteen of Boston's most notable
citizens. Among them were John Erving, a prominent Boston merchant; the Reverend Charles Chauncy, pastor of the
Tenth Congregational Church; and John Hancock, who would
later gain fame for his signature on the Declaration of Inde-
pendence. At the center of this group was His Excellency,
Thomas Hutchinson, governor of Massachusetts, with An-
drew Oliver, his lieutenant governor, close by his side.

Why had this august group been assembled? Why had it
seen fit to summon this young African girl, scarcely eighteen
years old, before it? This group of "the most respectable
Characters in *Boston*," as it would define itself, had assembled
to question closely the African adolescent on the slender sheaf
of poems that she claimed to have "written by herself." We
can only speculate on the nature of the questions posed to the
fledgling poet. Perhaps they asked her to identify and explain—for all to hear—exactly who were the Greek and Latin
gods and poets alluded to so frequently in her work. Perhaps
they asked her to conjugate a verb in Latin or even to trans-
late randomly selected passages from the Latin, which she
and her master, John Wheatley, claimed that she "had made
some Progress in." Or perhaps they asked her to recite from
memory key passages from the texts of John Milton and
Alexander Pope, the two poets by whom the African claimed
to be most directly influenced. We do not know.

We do know, however, that the African poet's responses
were more than sufficient to prompt the eighteen august
gentlemen to compose, sign, and publish a two-paragraph
"Attestation," an open letter "To the Publick" that prefaces
Phillis Wheatley's book and that reads in part:

> We whose Names are under-written, do assure the World,
> that the Poems specified in the following Page, were (as we

verily believe) written by Phillis, a young Negro Girl, who
was but a few Years since, brought an uncultivated Barbarian
from *Africa,* and has ever since been, and now is, under the
Disadvantage of serving as a Slave in a Family in this Town.
She has been examined by some of the best Judges, and is
thought qualified to write them.

So important was this document in securing a publisher for
Wheatley's poems that it forms the signal element in the pre-
fatory matter preceding her *Poems on Various Subjects, Religious and Moral,* published in London in 1773.

Without the published "Attestation," Wheatley's publisher
claimed, few would believe that an African could possibly
have written poetry all by herself. As the eighteen put the
matter clearly in their letter, "Numbers would be ready to
suspect they were not really the Writings of Phillis." Wheatley and her master, John Wheatley, had attempted to publish
a similar volume in 1772 in Boston, but Boston publishers
had been incredulous. One year later, "Attestation" in hand,
Phillis Wheatley and her master's son, Nathaniel Wheatley,
sailed for England, where they completed arrangements for
the publication of a volume of her poems with the aid of the
Countess of Huntington and the Earl of Dartmouth.

This curious anecdote, surely one of the oddest oral ex-
aminations on record, is only a tiny part of a larger, and
even more curious, episode in the Enlightenment. Since the
beginning of the sixteenth century, Europeans had wondered
aloud whether or not the African "species of men," as they
were most commonly called, *could* ever create formal literature, could ever master "the arts and sciences." If they could,
the argument ran, then the African variety of humanity was
fundamentally related to the European variety. If not, then
it seemed clear that the African was destined by nature to be
a slave. This was the burden shouldered by Phillis Wheatley

when she successfully defended herself and the authorship of her book against counterclaims and doubts.

Indeed, with her successful defense, Wheatley launched two traditions at once—the black American literary tradition *and* the black woman's literary tradition. If it is extraordinary that not just one but both of these traditions were founded simultaneously by a black woman—certainly an event unique in the history of literature—it is also ironic that this important fact of common, coterminous literary origins seems to have escaped most scholars.

That the progenitor of the black literary tradition was a woman means, in the most strictly literal sense, that all subsequent black writers have evolved in a matrilinear line of descent, and that each, consciously or unconsciously, has extended and revised a canon whose foundation was the poetry of a black woman. Early black writers seem to have been keenly aware of Wheatley's founding role, even if most of her white reviewers were more concerned with the implications of her race than her gender. Jupiter Hammon, for example, whose 1760 broadside "An Evening Thought. Salvation by Christ, With Penitential Cries" was the first individual poem published by a black American, acknowledged Wheatley's influence by selecting her as the subject of his second broadside, "An Address to Miss Phillis Wheatly [*sic*], Ethiopian Poetess, in Boston," which was published in Hartford in 1778. And George Moses Horton, the second African American to publish a book of poetry in English (1829), brought out in 1838 an edition of his *Poems By A Slave* bound together with Wheatley's work. Indeed, for fifty-six years, between 1773 and 1829, when Horton published *The Hope of Liberty*, Wheatley was the *only* black person to have published a book of imaginative literature in English. So central was this black woman's role in the shaping of the

African-American literary tradition that, as one historian has maintained, the history of the reception of Phillis Wheatley's poetry *is* the history of African-American literary criticism. Well into the nineteenth century, Wheatley and the black literary tradition were the same entity.

But Wheatley is not the only black woman writer who stands as a pioneering figure in African-American literature. Just as Wheatley gave birth to the genre of black poetry, Ann Plato was the first African American to publish a book of essays (1841) and Harriet E. Wilson was the first black person to publish a novel in the United States (1859).

Despite this pioneering role of black women in the tradition, however, many of their contributions before this century have been all but lost or unrecognized. As Hortense Spillers observed as recently as 1983,

> With the exception of a handful of autobiographical narratives from the nineteenth century, the black woman's realities are virtually suppressed until the period of the Harlem Renaissance and later. Essentially the black woman as artist, as intellectual spokesperson for her own cultural apprenticeship, has not existed before, for anyone. At the source of [their] own symbol-making task, [the community of black women writers] confronts, therefore, a tradition of work that is quite recent, its continuities, broken and sporadic.

Until now, it has been extraordinarily difficult to establish the formal connections between early black women's writing and that of the present, precisely because our knowledge of their work has been broken and sporadic. Phillis Wheatley, for example, while certainly the most reprinted and discussed poet in the tradition, is also one of the least understood. Ann Plato's seminal work, *Essays* (which includes biographies and poems), has not been reprinted since it was published a century and a half ago. And Harriet Wilson's *Our Nig,* her

compelling novel of a black woman's expanding consciousness in a racist Northern antebellum environment, never received even *one* review or comment at a time when virtually
all works written by black people were heralded by abolition-
ists as salient arguments against the existence of human slav-
ery. Many of the books reprinted in this set experienced a
similar fate, the most dreadful fate for an author: that of
being ignored then relegated to the obscurity of the rare book
section of a university library. We can only wonder how
many other texts in the black woman's tradition have been
lost to this generation of readers or remain unclassified or
uncatalogued and, hence, unread.

This was not always so, however. Black women writers
dominated the final decade of the nineteenth century, perhaps
spurred to publish by an 1886 essay entitled "The Coming
American Novelist," which was published in *Lippincott's
Monthly Magazine* and written by "A Lady From Philadelphia." This pseudonymous essay argued that the "Great
American Novel" would be written by a black person. Her
argument is so curious that it deserves to be repeated:

> When we come to formulate our demands of the Coming
> American Novelist, we will agree that he must be native-
> born. His ancestors may come from where they will, but we
> must give him a birthplace and have the raising of him.
> Still, the longer his family has been here the better he will
> represent us. Suppose he should have no country but ours,
> no traditions but those he has learned here, no longings apart
> from us, no future except in our future—the orphan of the
> world, he finds with us his home. And with all this, suppose
> he refuses to be fused into that grand conglomerate we call
> the "American type." With us, he is not of us. He is origi-
> nal, he has humor, he is tender, he is passive and fiery, he
> has been taught what we call justice, and he has his own
> opinion about it. He has suffered everything a poet, a dra-

matist, a novelist need suffer before he comes to have his lips anointed. And with it all he is in one sense a spectator, a little out of the race. How would these conditions go towards forming an original development? In a word, suppose the coming novelist is of African origin? When one comes to consider the subject, there is no improbability in it. One thing is certain,—our great novel will not be written by the typical American.

An atypical American, indeed. Not only would the great American novel be written by an African American, it would be written by an African-American *woman:*

> Yet farther: I have used the generic masculine pronoun because it is convenient; but Fate keeps revenge in store. It was a woman who, taking the wrongs of the African as her theme, wrote the novel that awakened the world to their reality, and why should not the coming novelist be a woman as well as an African? She—the woman of that race—has some claims on Fate which are not yet paid up.

It is these claims on fate that we seek to pay by publishing The Schomburg Library of Nineteenth-Century Black Women Writers.

This theme would be repeated by several black women authors, most notably by Anna Julia Cooper, a prototypical black feminist whose 1892 *A Voice From the South* can be considered to be one of the original texts of the black feminist movement. It was Cooper who first analyzed the fallacy of referring to "the Black man" when speaking of black people and who argued that just as white men cannot speak through the consciousness of black men, neither can black *men* "fully and adequately . . . reproduce the exact Voice of the Black Woman." Gender and race, she argues, cannot be conflated, except in the instance of a black woman's voice, and it is this voice which must be uttered and to which we must listen. As Cooper puts the matter so compellingly:

It is not the intelligent woman vs. the ignorant woman; nor the white woman vs. the black, the brown, and the red,—it is not even the cause of woman vs. man. Nay, 'tis woman's strongest vindication for speaking that *the world needs to hear her voice*. It would be subversive of every human interest that the cry of one-half the human family be stifled. Woman in stepping from the pedestal of statue-like inactivity in the domestic shrine, and daring to think and move and speak,—to undertake to help shape, mold, and direct the thought of her age, is merely completing the circle of the world's vision. Hers is every interest that has lacked an interpreter and a defender. Her cause is linked with that of every agony that has been dumb—every wrong that needs a voice.

It is no fault of man's that he has not been able to see truth from her standpoint. It does credit both to his head and heart that no greater mistakes have been committed or even wrongs perpetrated while she sat making tatting and snipping paper flowers. Man's own innate chivalry and the mutual interdependence of their interests have insured his treating her cause, in the main at least, as his own. And he is pardonably surprised and even a little chagrined, perhaps, to find his legislation not considered "perfectly lovely" in every respect. But in any case his work is only impoverished by her remaining dumb. The world has had to limp along with the wobbling gait and one-sided hesitancy of a man with one eye. Suddenly the bandage is removed from the other eye and the whole body is filled with light. It sees a circle where before it saw a segment. The darkened eye restored, every member rejoices with it.

The myopic sight of the darkened eye can only be restored when the full range of the black woman's voice, with its own special timbres and shadings, remains mute no longer.

Similarly, Victoria Earle Matthews, an author of short stories and essays, and a cofounder in 1896 of the National Association of Colored Women, wrote in her stunning essay,

"The Value of Race Literature" (1895), that "when the literature of our race is developed, it will of necessity be different in all essential points of greatness, true heroism and
real Christianity from what we may at the present time, for
convenience, call American literature." Matthews argued that
this great tradition of African-American literature would be
the textual outlet "for the unnaturally suppressed inner lives
which our people have been compelled to lead." Once these
"unnaturally suppressed inner lives" of black people are unveiled, no "grander diffusion of mental light" will shine more
brightly, she concludes, than that of the articulate African-
American woman:

> And now comes the question, What part shall we women
> play in the Race Literature of the future? . . . within the
> compass of one small journal ["Woman's Era"] we have struck
> out a new line of departure—a journal, a record of Race
> interests gathered from all parts of the United States, care-
> fully selected, moistened, winnowed and garnered by the ablest
> intellects of educated colored women, shrinking at no lofty
> theme, shirking no serious duty, aiming at every possible
> excellence, and determined to do their part in the future
> uplifting of the race.
>
> If twenty women, by their concentrated efforts in one lit-
> erary movement, can meet with such success as has engen-
> dered, planned out, and so successfully consummated this
> convention, what much more glorious results, what wider
> spread success, what grander diffusion of mental light will
> not come forth at the bidding of the enlarged hosts of women
> writers, already called into being by the stimulus of your
> efforts?
>
> And here let me speak one word for my journalistic sisters
> who have already entered the broad arena of journalism. Be-
> fore the "Woman's Era" had come into existence, no one
> except themselves can appreciate the bitter experience and sore

disappointments under which they have at all times been compelled to pursue their chosen vocations.

If their brothers of the press have had their difficulties to contend with, I am here as a sister journalist to state, from the fullness of knowledge, that their task has been an easy one compared with that of the colored woman in journalism.

Woman's part in Race Literature, as in Race building, is the most important part and has been so in all ages. . . . All through the most remote epochs she has done her share in literature. . . .

One of the most important aspects of this set is the republication of the salient texts from 1890 to 1910, which literary historians could well call the "Black Woman's Era." In addition to Mary Helen Washington's definitive edition of Cooper's *A Voice From the South,* we have reprinted two novels by Amelia Johnson, Frances Harper's *Iola Leroy,* two novels by Emma Dunham Kelley, Alice Dunbar-Nelson's two impressive collections of short stories, and Pauline Hopkins's three serialized novels as well as her monumental novel, *Contending Forces*—all published between 1890 and 1910. Indeed, black women published more works of fiction in these two decades than black men had published in the previous half century. Nevertheless, this great achievement has been ignored.

Moreover, the writings of nineteenth-century African-American women in general have remained buried in obscurity, accessible only in research libraries or in overpriced and poorly edited reprints. Many of these books have never been reprinted at all; in some instances only one or two copies are extant. In these works of fiction, poetry, autobiography, biography, essays, and journalism resides the mind of the nineteenth-century African-American woman. Until these works are made readily available to teachers and their students, a significant segment of the black tradition will remain silent.

Oxford University Press, in collaboration with the Schomburg Center for Research in Black Culture, is publishing thirty volumes of these compelling works, each of which contains an introduction by an expert in the field. The set includes such rare texts as Johnson's *The Hazeley Family* and *Clarence and Corinne*, Plato's *Essays*, the most complete edition of Phillis Wheatley's poems and letters, Emma Dunham Kelley's pioneering novel *Megda*, several previously unpublished stories and a novel by Alice Dunbar-Nelson, and the first collected volumes of Pauline Hopkins's three serialized novels and Frances Harper's poetry. We also present four volumes of poetry by such women as Henrietta Cordelia Ray, Adah Menken, Josephine Heard, and Maggie Johnson. Numerous slave and spiritual narratives, a newly discovered novel—*Four Girls at Cottage City*—by Emma Dunham Kelley (-Hawkins), and the first American edition of *Wonderful Adventures of Mrs. Seacole in Many Lands* are also among the texts included.

In addition to resurrecting the works of black women authors, it is our hope that this set will facilitate the resurrection of the African-American woman's literary tradition itself by unearthing its nineteenth-century roots. In the works of Nella Larsen and Jessie Fauset, Zora Neale Hurston and Ann Petry, Lorraine Hansberry and Gwendolyn Brooks, Paule Marshall and Toni Cade Bambara, Audre Lorde and Rita Dove, Toni Morrison and Alice Walker, Gloria Naylor and Jamaica Kincaid, these roots have branched luxuriantly. The eighteenth- and nineteenth-century authors whose works are presented in this set founded and nurtured the black women's literary tradition, which must be revived, explicated, analyzed, and debated before we can understand more completely the formal shaping of this tradition within a tradition, a coded literary universe through which, regrettably, we are only just beginning to navigate our way. As Anna Cooper said nearly one hundred years ago, we have been blinded by the loss of sight in one eye and have therefore been unable to detect the full *shape* of the African-American literary tradition.

Literary works configure into a tradition not because of some mystical collective unconscious determined by the biology of race or gender, but because writers read other writers and *ground* their representations of experience in models of language provided largely by other writers to whom they feel akin. It is through this mode of literary revision, amply evident in the *texts* themselves—in formal echoes, recast metaphors, even in parody—that a "tradition" emerges and defines itself.

This is formal bonding, and it is only through formal bonding that we can know a literary tradition. The collective publication of these works by black women now, for the first time, makes it possible for scholars and critics, male and female, black and white, to *demonstrate* that black women writers read, and revised, other black women writers. To demonstrate this set of formal literary relations is to demonstrate that sexuality, race, and gender are both the condition and the basis of *tradition*—but tradition as found in discrete acts of language use.

A word is in order about the history of this set. For the past decade, I have taught a course, first at Yale and then at Cornell, entitled "Black Woman and Their Fictions," a course that I inherited from Toni Morrison, who developed it in the mid-1970s for Yale's Program in Afro-American Studies. Although the course was inspired by the remarkable accomplishments of black women novelists since 1970, I gradually extended its beginning date to the late nineteenth century, studying Frances Harper's *Iola Leroy* and Anna Julia Cooper's *A Voice From the South,* both published in 1892. With the discovery of Harriet E. Wilson's seminal novel, *Our Nig* (1859), and Jean Yellin's authentication of Harriet Jacobs's brilliant slave narrative, *Incidents in the Life of a Slave Girl* (1861), a survey course spanning over a century and a quarter emerged.

But the discovery of *Our Nig,* as well as the interest in nineteenth-century black women's writing that this discovery generated, convinced me that even the most curious and diligent scholars knew very little of the extensive history of the creative writings of African-American women before 1900. Indeed, most scholars of African-American literature had never even read most of the books published by black women, simply because these books—of poetry, novels, short stories, essays, and autobiography—were mostly accessible only in rare book sections of university libraries. For reasons unclear to me even today, few of these marvelous renderings of the African-American woman's consciousness were reprinted in the late 1960s and early 1970s, when so many other texts of the African-American literary tradition were resurrected from the dark and silent graveyard of the out-of-print and were reissued in facsimile editions aimed at the hungry readership for canonical texts in the nascent field of black studies.

So, with the help of several superb research assistants—including David Curtis, Nicola Shilliam, Wendy Jones, Sam Otter, Janadas Devan, Suvir Kaul, Cynthia Bond, Elizabeth Alexander, and Adele Alexander—and with the expert advice of scholars such as William Robinson, William Andrews, Mary Helen Washington, Maryemma Graham, Jean Yellin, Houston A. Baker, Jr., Richard Yarborough, Hazel Carby, Joan R. Sherman, Frances Foster, and William French, dozens of bibliographies were used to compile a list of books written or narrated by black women mostly before 1910. Without the assistance provided through this shared experience of scholarship, the scholar's true legacy, this project would not have been conceived. As the list grew, I was struck by how very many of these titles that I, for example, had never even heard of, let alone read, such as Ann Plato's *Essays,* Louisa Picquet's slave narrative, or Amelia Johnson's two novels, *Clarence and Corinne* and *The Hazeley Family.* Through our research with the Black Periodical Fiction and Poetry Project (funded by NEH and the Ford Foundation), I also realized that several novels by black women, including three works of fiction by Pauline Hopkins, had been serialized in black periodicals, but had never been collected and published as books. Nor had the several books of poetry published by black women, such as the prolific Frances E. W. Harper, been collected and edited. When I discovered still another "lost" novel by an African-American woman (*Four Girls at Cottage City,* published in 1898 by Emma Dunham Kelley-Hawkins), I decided to attempt to edit a collection of reprints of these works and to publish them as a "library" of black women's writings, in part so that I could read them myself.

Convincing university and trade publishers to undertake this project proved to be a difficult task. Despite the commercial success of *Our Nig* and of the several reprint series of women's works (such as Virago, the Beacon Black Women Writers Series, and Rutgers' American Women Writers Series), several presses rejected the project as "too large," "too limited," or as "commercially unviable." Only two publishers recognized the viability and the import of the project and, of these, Oxford's commitment to publish the titles simultaneously as a set made the press's offer irresistible.

While attempting to locate original copies of these exceedingly rare books, I discovered that most of the texts were housed at the Schomburg Center for Research in Black Culture, a branch of The New York Public Library, under the direction of Howard Dodson. Dodson's infectious enthusiasm for the project and his generous collaboration, as well as that of his stellar staff (especially Diana Lachatanere, Sharon Howard, Ellis Haizip, Richard Newman, and Betty Gubert), led to a joint publishing initiative that produced this set as part of the Schomburg's major fund-raising campaign. Without Dodson's foresight and generosity of spirit, the set would not have materialized. Without William P. Sisler's masterful editorship at Oxford and his staff's careful attention to detail, the set would have remained just another grand idea that tends to languish in a scholar's file cabinet.

I would also like to thank Dr. Michael Winston and Dr. Thomas C. Battle, Vice-President of Academic Affairs and the Director of the Moorland-Spingarn Research Center (respectively) at Howard University, for their unending encouragement, support, and collaboration in this project, and Esme E. Bhan at Howard for her meticulous research and bibliographical skills. In addition, I would like to acknowledge the aid of the staff at the libraries of Duke University, Cornell University (especially Tom Weissinger and Donald Eddy), the Boston Public Library, the Western Reserve Historical Society, the Library of Congress, and Yale University. Linda Robbins, Marion Osmun, Sarah Flanagan, and Gerard Case, all members of the staff at Oxford, were extraordinarily effective at coordinating, editing, and producing the various segments of each text in the set. Candy Ruck, Nina de Tar, and Phillis Molock expertly typed reams of correspondence and manuscripts connected to the project.

I would also like to express my gratitude to my colleagues who edited and introduced the individual titles in the set. Without their attention to detail, their willingness to meet strict deadlines, and their sheer enthusiasm for this project, the set could not have been published. But finally and ultimately, I would hope that the publication of the set would help to generate even more scholarly interest in the black women authors whose work is presented here. Struggling against the seemingly insurmountable barriers of racism *and* sexism, while often raising families and fulfilling full-time professional obligations, these women managed nevertheless to record their thoughts and feelings and to *testify* to all who dare read them that the will to harness the power of collective endurance and survival is the will to write.

The Schomburg Library of Nineteenth-Century Black Women Writers is dedicated in memory of Pauline Augusta Coleman Gates, who died in the spring of 1987. It was she who inspired in me the love of learning and the love of literature. I have encountered in the books of this set no will more determined, no courage more noble, no mind more sublime, no self more celebratory of the achievements of all African-American women, and indeed of life itself, than her own.

A NOTE FROM
THE SCHOMBURG CENTER

Howard Dodson

The Schomburg Center for Research in Black Culture, The New York Public Library, is pleased to join with Dr. Henry Louis Gates and Oxford University Press in presenting The Schomburg Library of Nineteenth-Century Black Women Writers. This thirty-volume set includes the work of a generation of black women whose writing has only been available previously in rare book collections. The materials reprinted in twenty-four of the thirty volumes are drawn from the unique holdings of the Schomburg Center.

A research unit of The New York Public Library, the Schomburg Center has been in the forefront of those institutions dedicated to collecting, preserving, and providing access to the records of the black past. In the course of its two generations of acquisition and conservation activity, the Center has amassed collections totaling more than 5 million items. They include over 100,000 bound volumes, 85,000 reels and sets of microforms, 300 manuscript collections containing some 3.5 million items, 300,000 photographs and extensive holdings of prints, sound recordings, film and videotape, newspapers, artworks, artifacts, and other book and nonbook materials. Together they vividly document the history and cultural heritages of people of African descent worldwide.

Though established some sixty-two years ago, the Center's book collections date from the sixteenth century. Its oldest item, an Ethiopian Coptic Tunic, dates from the eighth or ninth century. Rare materials, however, are most available for the nineteenth-century African-American experience. It is from these holdings that the majority of the titles selected for inclusion in this set are drawn.

The nineteenth century was a formative period in African-American literary and cultural history. Prior to the Civil War, the majority of black Americans living in the United States were held in bondage. Law and practice forbade teaching them to read or write. Even after the war, many of the impediments to learning and literary productivity remained. Nevertheless, black men and women of the nineteenth century persevered in both areas. Moreover, more African Americans than we yet realize turned their observations, feelings, social viewpoints, and creative impulses into published works. In time, this nineteenth-century printed record included poetry, short stories, histories, novels, autobiographies, social criticism, and theology, as well as economic and philosophical treatises. Unfortunately, much of this body of literature remained, until very recently, relatively inaccessible to twentieth-century scholars, teachers, creative artists, and others interested in black life. Prior to the late 1960s, most Americans (black as well as white) had never heard of these nineteenth-century authors, much less read their works.

The civil rights and black power movements created unprecedented interest in the thought, behavior, and achievements of black people. Publishers responded by revising traditional texts, introducing the American public to a new generation of African-American writers, publishing a variety of thematic anthologies, and reprinting a plethora of "classic texts" in African-American history, literature, and art. The reprints usually appeared as individual titles or in a series of bound volumes or microform formats.

The Schomburg Center, which has a long history of supporting publishing that deals with the history and culture of Africans in diaspora, became an active participant in many of the reprint revivals of the 1960s. Since hard copies of original printed works are the preferred formats for producing facsimile reproductions, publishers frequently turned to the Schomburg Center for copies of these original titles. In addition to providing such material, Schomburg Center staff members offered advice and consultation, wrote introductions, and occasionally entered into formal copublishing arrangements in some projects.

Most of the nineteenth-century titles reprinted during the 1960s, however, were by and about black men. A few black women were included in the longer series, but works by lesser known black women were generally overlooked. The Schomburg Library of Nineteenth-Century Black Women Writers is both a corrective to these previous omissions and an important contribution to African-American literary history in its own right. Through this collection of volumes, the thoughts, perspectives, and creative abilities of nineteenth-century African-American women, as captured in books and pamphlets published in large part before 1910, are again being made available to the general public. The Schomburg Center is pleased to be a part of this historic endeavor.

I would like to thank Professor Gates for initiating this project. Thanks are due both to him and Mr. William P. Sisler of Oxford University Press for giving the Schomburg Center an opportunity to play such a prominent role in the set. Thanks are also due to my colleagues at The New York Public Library and the Schomburg Center, especially Dr. Vartan Gregorian, Richard De Gennaro, Paul Fasana, Betsy Pinover, Richard Newman, Diana Lachatanere, Glenderlyn Johnson, and Harold Anderson for their assistance and support. I can think of no better way of demonstrating than in this set the role the Schomburg Center plays in assuring that the black heritage will be available for future generations.

CONTENTS

The Collected Works of
Effie Waller Smith

INTRODUCTION

David Deskins
with Jennifer Kovach

Effie Waller Smith left little record of her existence. There are no diaries or journals that might allow one to sift through her thoughts and learn about her. There are only her three volumes of verse, her three short stories, and the few poems that she wrote for exclusive literary magazines. All published during an intense thirteen-year period, these works are the signs of what we might call her literary success and her life. They testify to her desires and ambitions as a creative writer, and yet they remained largely unacknowledged, even by those close to her. She died in total obscurity.

As her life story unfolded itself to me, I became aware of just how unfitting this obscurity was for a poet who had once written of the yearning "For an illustr'ous name,/ For the applause and praise of men,"[1] and who had indeed found a measure of success in direct competition with the best of America's authors. Even more unfitting is the fact that Effie Waller Smith, who lived to the ripe age of eighty, stopped writing—or in any case, stopped publishing—at the age of thirty-eight.

I first learned of Effie Waller Smith through Bruce Brown, a professor at Pikeville College where I studied English from 1967 to 1971. Knowing of my interest in poetry, Brown loaned me a copy of Waller's first collection, *Songs of the Months,* in 1972 to read for insight into the poetry of my own native soil of eastern Kentucky, which Waller so revered in her work. I read the volume and returned it to Brown, but Waller and her writing remained with me. It did strike me at the time, however, that a black woman writing lyrical ballads and other forms of verse in eastern Kentucky, hardly a hotbed for traditional poetry at the turn of the century, was unusual. Beyond that I did not categorize what I had read; I only appreciated the good writing, somewhat mystified by its existence.

It was in 1987 that I began an effort to reconstruct the life of Effie Waller Smith (in as much as was possible) and to determine the extent of her literary career. Fifteen years after my initial encounter with "Miss Effie," as she had been known and as I too had begun to call her, I decided that she was a writer of unusual talent who had failed to enter the permanent literary record. Further, I felt that her writings were worthy and that she was important, both from an artistic and a historical perspective. I concluded that because of the difficulty black writers encountered in trying to publish their work, let alone achieve any literary fame, her voice had been confined mostly to a small, local audience, and that this condition ultimately silenced her. As an inheritor of her legacy, I thought that it was my responsibility to write about her life and release her song, as much as could be done.

I gained much of my early information about Waller through oral histories, which I later tried to document. Brown had informed me that he had heard of Waller through his parents and grandparents. His grandparents, who lived on Raccoon Creek, a section of the Pikeville community in eastern Kentucky where only white people lived at that time, had described the Waller family, who lived on nearby, racially mixed Chloe Creek, as "prominent." His grandparents also described Effie Waller Smith as a poet who had published books, though they did not have copies of them. Intrigued by this bit of local history, Brown, then a high school student, began his own search for Waller's books among his friends. Sylvia Auxier, one of his teachers, discovered Waller's *Songs of the Months* and *Rhymes from the Cumberland* in her mother-in-law's attic; these were subsequently presented to Brown as a gift.[2]

Brown's initial interest established Effie Waller Smith as a genuine subject of research that has only recently been recognized for its singular importance. Following Brown's lead, in 1980 Alice Kinder, a columnist for the *Appalachian News Express* (Pikeville), wrote two biographical articles on Waller after reading the two books that Brown held. Kinder elicited a biographical sketch from Ruth Smith, Effie's adopted daughter (formerly Ruth Ratliff of Pikeville), whom Kinder had located in Neenah, Wisconsin. Ruth Smith also gave important information to me during two taped interviews in 1987 and several times later when subsequent questions arose in my attempt to gather all available data concerning her adoptive mother. Much of the biography in the discussion that follows has been reconstructed from the stories that Ruth Smith has so kindly shared with me.

One of the few surviving documents containing information on Effie Waller Smith's parents is an article written by Jay Fraley in the April 2, 1926 issue of the *Pike County News:*

> While General Ratliff sympathized with the Southern cause he also sympathized with the colored people. On one occasion [in 1860] a man named Slone who lived on the Levisa Fork above Pikeville had his slaves sold at auction. General Ratliff owned no slaves but because he hated to see the family of slaves separated he went out and tried to buy them. He was outbidden but succeeded in buying the mother and daughter and kept them together until the mother's death. The daughter

remained with the Ratliff family in Pikeville until she married Uncle Frank Waller, a former slave from Spottyslvania County, Virginia.

That mother was Effie Waller Smith's maternal grandmother and the daughter was Sibbie, Effie's mother. Their experiences typify those of many slave families during and after the Civil War. At the present time, no other information about Waller's maternal family has been located.

A little more is known about her father, Frank Waller. He was born in 1845 on a plantation on the North Anna River in east Virginia. Called Cedar Point, the plantation was a large and successful operation owned by the important Waller family.[3] Records of Frank Waller first appear in the 1870 census, when he was twenty-five, and in courthouse documents for that same year. No record of when he came to Kentucky has been found. It is known that he was very successful in his capacities as a farmer, blacksmith, and businessman who speculated in property and who accumulated a sizable estate by the time of his death. Though not formally educated, he was known to be an effective manager who valued education.

Frank Waller and Sibbie Ratliff married in 1873 and established a farm on Chloe Creek about four miles from Pikeville. Born first to the two were Alfred in 1874 and Rosa in 1875. Their third child, Effie, was born on January 6, 1879. The youngest Waller child, Marvin, who appears frequently in Effie's poetry, was born in 1882 but died in his early twenties.[4]

According to Ruth Smith,

> Effie Waller had a very congenial home life. Her parents read to her, what little they could being [former] slaves and not having much of a chance. Her parents provided a deeply

religious background. . . . She said they did a lot of things together, berry picking. . . . They would gather about the fire and pop corn and her father would tell stories about his slave days. Evidently he had a very good master.[5]

It was this supportive environment that enabled the Waller children to become teachers of "unusual mentality," according to the author of the introduction to *Songs of the Months*. In the 1890s Alfred and Rosa both attended Kentucky Normal School for Colored Persons in Frankfort, Kentucky.[6] Several years older than Effie, they served as her early mentors who gave her books and poetry of a traditional nature. She, bright and anxious to learn, helped by those of her kin, did the rest. She attended the local segregated school system, achieving the highest education she could get there (up through the eighth grade), and then she went to the Kentucky Normal School For Colored Persons in 1900 and 1901. After completing the teacher training program, she spent the next sixteen years writing and teaching (off and on) in schools in her hometown and eastern Tennessee.[7]

In 1902 several of Pikeville's residents recognized both Effie Waller's potential as a poet (by then, she had published some poems in local newspapers)[8] and the racist barriers she would confront in realizing her talent more fully. They acted on her behalf, and it is likely that they gave her considerable financial support. *Songs of the Months* was published two years later. Its introduction, which constitutes an appeal to give this new young poet a reading despite the situation of her birth, is penned by Mary Elliott Flanery, at that time a Pikeville resident and later an important figure in Kentucky's political history.[9] Several of the poems in the volume are dedicated to Flanery and others whose kindness Waller wanted to acknowledge.

In February 1908 Effie Waller married Charles Smith in
Kentucky. Charles had been Effie's classmate at Colored
School District "A" in Pikeville and two years her senior.
Though they were always close (see "On Recevving a Souvenir Post-card" in *Rhymes from the Cumberland,*) they failed
to marry early in their lives, and when married, they did not
remain together very long. In fact, according to the 1900
census, Charles was first married to Louisa Smith and had
one child. He divorced Louisa in 1904, the same year that
Effie married Lyss Cockrell, likely a transient worker on the
railroads. She divorced him less than a year later after he had
left her to live with another woman.

During the same month that she married Charles, Effie
experienced an intense burst of success that lasted until December 1909. She published two volumes of poems—*Rhymes
from the Cumberland* and *Rosemary and Pansies*—and had three
short stories as well as two poems appear in national literary
magazines. Then it seems that her writing efforts slowed.
Though she was only thirty years of age when *Rosemary and
Pansies* came out in late 1909, only two more poems of hers
were published in major national outlets. One of these, "The
Faded Blossoms," appeared in the *Independent* in its July 20,
1911 issue. A sonnet, it is one of her most powerful, artistic
statements about life. Just a few months previous to the
poem's publication, her husband Charles, a deputy sheriff
from whom she had been separated since July 1908, was
murdered while serving a warrant in rural Pike County. The
death certificate terms his death a "homicide." Yet six months
later the parties accused were found innocent in a trial that
lasted less than a day. Effie Waller Smith did not appear in
print again until 1917 when "Autumn Winds" was published
in *Harper's Magazine*. Thereafter her work disappeared from
the public record altogether.

A few years after the death of her father in 1916, Effie and her mother Sibbie left Pikeville to join a religious sect called the Metropolitan Church Association in Waukesha, Wisconsin. Fundamentalist Methodist, the sect operated a commune in Waukesha, and Effie and Sibbie lived on it for several years. Becoming dissatisfied in 1924, they left the commune, and Effie joined the local Methodist Episcopal Church where she was an active member for many years. She continued to live with her mother until Sibbie's death in 1927, at which time her brother Alfred, a retired railroad worker, moved in until his death in 1933.

Waller herself remained in Wisconsin for the rest of her life, returning to Pikeville only to adopt Ruth Ratliff, the daughter of one of Effie's former friends and students, Polly Mullins Ratliff, who died in 1927. Ruth, who lived in sight of a white school but was not allowed to attend it, was seventeen years old. She had difficulty making the four-mile walk to and from the segregated school she was forced to attend, making her presence there quite irregular. Then Effie took Ruth to Waukesha, Ruth began school, though much older than the other students, and she eventually graduated from high school and college in 1944. She began teaching in Neenah, Wisconsin, about one hundred miles from Waukesha and her adoptive mother.

In the early 1930s Waller constructed an enormous rock garden with hundreds of different varieties of blooming plants, flowers, and shrubs. A stationery box containing poems written until the time of her death reveals that she continued a very private interest in poetry throughout her life, while her garden became her form of public expression. She kept track of the visitors to her garden in a ledger that Ruth Ratliff Smith now holds. Thousands of people from near and far walked through the garden each year. But in 1950 Effie's health began to fail, and without the strength to keep up the garden, she sold her home in Waukesha and moved to Neenah to live with Ruth. In 1960, just four days short of her eighty-first birthday, Effie Waller Smith died in Neenah and is buried there. Her tombstone says E. W. Smith, 1879–1960. And nothing more.

It is difficult to assess Effie Waller Smith's work based on its critical reception. At the time that she was publishing, a singular mention was made of her in Reverend J. J. Pipkin's book, *The History of a Rising Race: The Negro in Revelation, in History and in Citizenship,* a study of the contributions of African Americans in the United States and the world in "Arms, Arts, Letter, The Pulpit, The Forum, The School, The Marts of Trade" through the year 1902.[10] Pipkin includes and highlights some of those known to him with promise to credit the race in future years. In Chapter 5, a section devoted to "The Negro in Literature and the Fine Arts," he summarizes the contributions of African Americans and others in this area. There follow six biographies, five of which describe such living authors (in 1902) as Paul Laurence Dunbar, Charles W. Chesnutt, and J. Corrothers, while one concerns Phillis Wheatley, who died in 1784. Along with the living authors are the unknowns Inez C. Parker and Effie Waller, whose inclusion with the likes of Dunbar, Corrothers, and Chesnutt tells us something about Pipkin's critical view of her work.[11]

The only other contemporaneous endorsement of Waller's work that has been found to date is embedded in the introduction to *Songs of the Months.* Author Mary Elliott Flanery's critical authority comes from her position in Kentucky society. Her approval of Waller's poetry is strengthened by her use of a poem written for Effie by the Rev. Peter Clay, an author of considerable local repute:

Yet God with music touched the singer's heart;
And thoughts in liquid measure
Doth flow out like a treasure,
To charm us with the poet's mystic arts.

Flanery also uses a long quote from the New York critic Mr. S. G. Clow, who was the proprietor of the company with which Waller published her first two books. Clow's comment suggests that an interest in Waller's poetry could be generated because of its subject matter, which he quite narrowly defines as "poems written close to nature's heart! . . . from the dear old Southland," and because her work "will do much to dissolve the foolish prejudice of color, and to prove that poetic genius is the heritage of their race."

Clow's projections can be substantiated as far as "practical" criticism goes. Waller climbed her way up the mainstream literary ladder by publishing first with local papers, then with a vanity press, then with national magazines, and then with a small, competitive Boston firm. Thus it is the physical evidence that serves as the critical "commentary" on her work and that seems to supersede the lack of formal recognition. It is entirely possible that we, in this age of information and rampant text production, misunderstand the nature of literary reputation at the turn of the century. Perhaps that misunderstanding, among other factors, is what makes Waller's place in the history of American literature difficult to determine.

Current literary commentary is equally sparse. Ann Allen Shockley does include *Songs of the Months* and *Rhymes from the Cumberland* in her book, *Afro-American Women Writers 1746–1933: An Anthology and Critical Guide*,[12] but provides no commentary. Jim Wayne Miller, author and literary historian, has written a short article for the spring 1989 issue of *Open Eye*, a magazine which mainly circulates within a popular audience in Kentucky, that contextualizes Waller's short story writing within the "Local Color" school of American writing. Perhaps someday a fuller account that attempts to synthesize the effect of region, race, and biography on Waller's writing will be rendered.

SONGS OF THE MONTHS

Songs of the Months was published in New York in 1904 by the Broadway Publishing Company, a vanity press that was used by many authors of the day. It is likely that *Songs* was distributed to certain editors and critics in an effort to make Effie Waller's talents known to them.[13] The 110 poems included in the collection comprise the poetry of her youth through her twenty-third year. Though these early poems are not of the same quality as those of John Greenleaf Whittier or William Cullen Bryant, they are entertaining and might well have pleased a popular audience of the time.

The introductory poem, "To the Reader," certainly one of the most expressive, artistic efforts in *Songs,* is an example of both the content and form of much of Waller's early writing. Technically, her poetic writing consists of versified sentiment with some figurative language. In this poem, the poet wishes to present her readers with the beauty of nature by writing a beautifully complex rhyme scheme of *a a a b c d c*. She writes descriptions of the full scope of the seasons in Kentucky, giving two instances in which something is personified. The tension in the poem develops out of the poet's desire to be at one with nature and at the same time a student of school learning. Waller, throughout her writing at least, was able to accept other such contradictory elements into her vision of the proper way to lead one's life. A notable example is the poem "Somebody's Father" in which she expresses grief over the death of a Union soldier.

The affinity that Smith felt toward nature cannot be downplayed. According to Alice Kinder, Waller became known in Pike County as "the singing poet of the Cumberlands." One of her former students in Pikeville recalled that she often sang to her class and that "if it was a particularly pretty day she was liable to turn class out early and head for that mountain over there, and spend the rest of the day walking looking at the birds and the flowers."[14] In Waller's poems, nature inspires the artist; at times nature is personified; and occasionally some aspect of nature becomes a figure. In her short stories, however, the importance of nature is superseded by a profound religious morality that drives her narrative.

Apart from nature, the poems in *Songs* cover other themes as well, offering a wide spectrum of topics that were common among authors writing in a Victorian style. A good many poems reflect a very high opinion of America and the patriotism of their author. Poems like "Remember the Maine," "Washington," "Yankee Doodle," and others could have been written by any patriotic American citizen of the day. Religion is a second topic, though it is not as dominant as in her later works. And love is a third theme, perhaps the most important in the collection.

Also prominent is a grouping of poems dealing with each month of the year. These, obviously early efforts and obviously special to Waller, are characteristic of her cyclic perspective on life; her poetry constantly embodies a simultaneous looking forward toward death and backward into her childhood. These poems inspired the name of the volume.

As historical documents, some poems depict life on the Cumberland Mountains at the turn of the century and in particular reveal what Waller's own life was like. Some of these include "Berrying Time," "The Corn-husking," "The 'Possum Hunt," "Decoration Day," "The Colored Soldiers of the Spanish-American War," and "Apple Sauce and Chicken Fried."

Race was a subject that only occasionally surfaced in her writing. A handful of poems out of the 110 in *Songs* indicates that she was interested in writing about race but not devoted to it as a subject. The poem "Answer to Verses Addressed to Me by Peter Clay" makes a strong statement about her understanding of the oppressive conditions under which she wrote:

> For 'tis the genius of the soul
>   (Though underneath a skin
> Of dusky hue its fire may burn)
>   Your unfeigned praises win.
>
> Oh, that the earth had more of beings
>   With generous minds like yours,
> Who alike, true worth and honor
>   To the black and white secures.
>
> Accept, dear poet, then, my thanks
>   For your glowing words of praise,
> For the simple, homely, faulty rhymes
>   Of my early girlhood days.

She was hopeful that equality would come to all people, but a clearly delineated racial theme disappeared as her writing continued.

RHYMES FROM THE CUMBERLAND

Rhymes from the Cumberland—published in 1909, again by the Broadway Publishing Company of New York—contains poetry written between 1903 and 1908 before Effie Waller's marriage to Charles Smith. It represents a watershed period in her writing where she combines her delight in nature with what would become a consuming interest in religion. The sixteen poems in Part I, most of which were written between 1903 and 1905, take the reader on a poetic tour of the Cumberland Mountains. The style is much like that found in *Songs of the Months* (a few poems in *Songs* reappear in *Rhymes*), with traditional ballads rhyming *a b c b*. Part II, however, is a loose collection of twenty-four poems that reveal Waller's employment of more complex rhythmic and stanzaic patterns than those used in her previous work.

Many of the poems in Part I, the Cumberland series, are about the "Breaks," an area in the mountains that is located twenty miles south of Pikeville, partly in Kentucky and partly in Virginia. Waller's poetry captures the rugged beauty of the area, as do the photographs included in this section of the book. Waller herself was a frequent visitor to the Breaks where the Big Sandy River had cut through the Pine Mountain fault line over the course of the last 250 million years. A sixteen-hundred-foot-deep gorge, the deepest east of the Mississippi River, is the drastic result, rising high above both sides of the river for many miles. Sheer cliffs and outcrops dominate the area overlooking the river, serving as open invitation for a lover of nature and beauty.[15] It is thought that Waller spent several extended sessions exploring the Breaks; her poems indicate she was enamored with the area.[16]

But as much as Waller loved nature, her visits to the Breaks may have been prompted by a deeper need for solitude and refuge. Her Pikeville home may well have been a good place for her and her family to be, as good as any in the country. Her father's success as a businessman indicates he was able to gain the respect of a majority of Pikeville's residents. It is a fact the Wallers were prominent members of the community.[17] But it is also doubtful that life in Pikeville was easy. To one as sensitive and perceptive as Effie Waller Smith, discrimination, even in a relatively benign atmosphere, would be upsetting. The turn of the century has been described as one of the most difficult times for the African-American minority in post-Civil War America, perhaps the nadir of their experience in this country.[18] Evidence of intense racial prejudice appeared on the front pages of the *Big Sandy Times*, the most significant regional weekly newspaper of the period.[19] Its editors often printed graphic accounts of lynching and other brutalities in the deep South— accounts by "reporters" who took devilish glee in rendering the details of their "news." The newspaper did not, however, report violence against African Americans in eastern Kentucky.

It is possible to speculate that the matchless beauty of the Breaks enabled Waller to escape from the real world of segregation, prejudice, and racial hatred and from all those who viewed her and members of her race as less than human. Since most of the poems in Part I of *Rhymes* were written during a difficult time of her life—her brother Marvin died in 1903, and she divorced Lyss Cockrell in 1905—the Breaks also could have provided some solace from great personal loss.

The poems in Part II alternate between romantic recollections and ruminations on the viability of religion. In *Songs of the Months*, a description of nature is allowed to dominate a poem until the very end when a religious sentiment enters. In *Rhymes from the Cumberland*, religious sentiment appears in most poems from the very beginning.

Some very personal poems in Part II concern Waller's relationship with Charles Smith. The poems about Smith include "On Receiving a Souvenir Post-card," "When You Are With Me," "A Recollection," "In the Years that Are to

Come," and "The Maples' Leaves Were Scarlet," but many
of the romantic poems focus on an unspecified lover.

Several poems indicate that Waller was not in Pikeville
when they were written and that her stays away from home
were extensive. Two of these, "On Receiving a Souvenir
Post-card" and "A Meadow Brook," make explicit references
to her Kentucky home, while many others treat the theme of
the loss of a loved one or of a happy childhood.

The final poem in *Rhymes*, "Lines written on the fly-leaf
. . . ," was written in 1904 and penned in on a blank page
of the copy of *Songs of the Months* that Waller presented to
Mary Elliott Flanery. It is the only poem in *Rhymes* that
mentions race, and it leaves little doubt about Waller's level
of self-knowledge as an African American living in the
mountains of Kentucky and in American society. Waller's
endorsement of Flanery is an ardent statement about her own
perception of the status of her race:

> As your eager eyes peruse
>   These pages over and again
> These verses sent me by the muse
>   I'd have you know that not in vain,
> You wrote those sincere words of praise
>   Of me who sprang from humble birth,
> Sprang from a race down trod and low,
>   Cursed, abused, despised of earth.

These lines, however, also indicate the resolve with which
Waller sought to challenge this dictum through her poetry.
The poem thus closes:

> A heart more generous than your own
> To fre[e]dom and to human kind
>   The flight of years have never known,
> Have never, never dared to find.
>   *Live long your principles to prove.*

"THE TEMPTING OF PETER STILES" AND OTHER WORKS PUBLISHED IN NATIONAL MAGAZINES

In February 1908 "The Tempting of Peter Stiles," a short story written under the name of Effie Smith, appeared in *Putnam's Monthly*. Further, according to the *Reader's Guide to Periodicals*, Effie Smith published a poem, "Benignant Death," and another short story, "A Son of Sorrow," in the December 1908 issue of *Putnam's Monthly*. She also published a poem titled "The Shepherds' Vision" in the December 24, 1908 issue of the *Independent*. These four significant literary achievements were followed by another short story by Effie Smith, "The Judgment of Roxenie," in the June 1909 issue of *Putnam's Monthly*, and the two 1908 poems—"Benignant Death" and "The Shepherds' Vision"—were included in *Rosemary and Pansies*, published under the name of Effie Smith in December 1909. According to the best possible information, there were no other Effie Smiths active and publishing at this time.

In all three stories, Waller presents a character who is forced to make a decision between improving his or her own situation and maintaining the code of some religious or moral system. "The Tempting of Peter Stiles," like the other two stories, is set in the mountains, most likely in east Tennessee. Peter Stiles, a sinner, and Deacon Gregg have a number of encounters as they attempt to work out the boundaries of their Christian relationship. Waller spends less time on the religious aspect of life in "A Son of Sorrow." In this story, the protagonist, Benoni Harwood, must decide whether his love for a woman is more important than his respect for God's rule, but the story focuses less on his dilemma than on the mountain community's group dynamics and folk wisdom. In "The Judgment of Roxenie," Waller suggests that what is right and wrong depends on the context and that ultimately self-indictment is the only way that can convince one to take the proper path in life.

I believe that in these later publishing efforts Waller kept, or was forced to keep, her race a secret. "The Tempting of Peter Stiles" is the only story of the three in which it is possible to interpret some aspect of the writing as having to do with the black experience. The story begins:

> To be the black sheep of a respectable flock is not the worst fate. If one has good blood in one's veins, it may sometime assert itself, in spite of one's individual misdoing; but to be the ignoble scion of a long and worthless ancestry has an element of hopelessness to it.

The above excerpt represents the very first words by Effie Waller Smith ever seen by a national audience. Was it chance that allowed so many allusions to creep in that might carry possible double meanings beyond the story about Peter Stiles? Within the bounds of this simple, fifty-one-word sentence, Waller makes reference to color (black), the quality of one's blood, a worthless ancestry, and an element of hopelessness. The meaning of these words is not limited to a universal story of redemption and is designed by an active mind to make two distinct and separate statements.

ROSEMARY AND PANSIES

The key to understanding the literary career of Effie Waller Smith may lie in the fact that very few, or perhaps no one at all, knew the full extent of her publishing. Bruce Brown's teacher, Sylvia Auxier, indicated that she knew Waller had written a third book besides *Songs of the Months* and *Rhymes from the Cumberland* but that she did not know its name.[20] This reference eventually led to my discovery of the third book, *Rosemary and Pansies,* in September 1987 when Rob Aiken, a research librarian at the Margaret I. King Library at the University of Kentucky, took the names that Waller might have used and ran them through the national network of libraries linked by computer. When the name Effie Smith was introduced to the computer, *Rosemary and Pansies* appeared on the screen.

In addition, the collection was brought out by a reputable publisher of some of the finest poetry of the period, the Gorham Press of Boston, Massachusetts. When Gorham's editor, Richard G. Badger, filed the copyright application for *Rosemary and Pansies* with the Library of Congress in December 1909, he listed the volume's author as Effie Smith of Baileyton, Tennessee. As noted, one of the volume's poems, "The Shepherds' Vision," had previously appeared in the *Independent* in 1908, though in a line following the poem, the magazine misspelled Baileyton as "Baileytown." The typographical error is slight. Clearly, Effie Smith, author of *Rosemary and Pansies,* was the same Effie Smith who now published in national magazines. It could even be postulated that Badger took Smith's national success into account when he accepted *Rosemary and Pansies* for publication.

The poetic forms employed in *Rosemary and Pansies* are similar to many that Waller used in the past except that they are far more polished. Many are examples of artistic perfection as they operate within convention (the combination of rhyme scheme, meter, and form) to develop mood and pleasingly deliver her message. Eight sonnets are included, but also prominent are seven "songs" in the simple *a b c b* scheme that Waller preferred in previous collections.

The tone of the volume is different from that of her earlier two books, however. Many of the poems are somber and subdued yet definite and conclusive as they examine issues and situations of life. There is a mood maintained throughout that sometimes delves into the mystical. Upbeat deviations are rare. Within *Rosemary and Pansies* are poems that reflect the maturation of Waller's poetic response to the difficulties she encountered in her life over the years. In July 1908 she filed for divorce from Charles; this, in conjunction with a continuing mourning over the loss of her brother and the death of her infant child late in 1908 or early in 1909, may account for the "aloneness" so apparent in the volume. It is an aloneness akin to that evidenced by Emily Dickinson in many of her writings. Indeed, in its reflections on personal loss, *Rosemary and Pansies* is a study of death much in the fashion of Dickinson's intense efforts to probe the idea and limits of death. Still, Waller's treatment differs from Dickinson's in that the former maintains a firm religious option and resolve throughout this last collection of her work.

In spite of the fact that there are no explicit references to race in *Rosemary and Pansies*, it is possible to establish that its author was African American. "A Mountain Graveyard" contains in its third stanza a description of certain grave decorations:

> There, too, scattered o'er the grass
> Of the graves, are bits of glass
> That with white shells mingled lie.
> Smile not, ye who pass them by,
> For the love that placed them there
> Deemed that they were things most fair.

Decorating graves with broken glass and sea shells (among other things) is an African-American cultural practice; the author, proud of her cultural heritage, dares anyone to "smile."[21]

"Benignant Death" also addresses the issue of race through the issue of death. Waller asks that without death,

> Would not life's long sordidness
> On our spirits pall,
> If our years should last forever,
> And the earth were all?

In the preceding stanza, she makes her reference to death socially specific, asking

> When would man's injustice cease
> Did not stern Death bring
> Those who cheated and oppressed
> To their reckoning?

Another question could be asked of Smith herself: What was the nature of her oppression? Did she experience and suffer oppression daily in a personal way? It is certain that she did for the lucidity and strength of message in this poem indicates that oppression was a subject to which she had given a good deal of thought and study. And it could be asked: Who were those who cheated and oppressed her? Who were those that made death almost a welcome option to her personal suffering?

THE LAST PUBLISHED POEM

In the September 1917 issue of *Harper's Magazine* is found Effie Waller Smith's finale, a sonnet called "Autumn Winds":

> O autumn winds, with voices far away,
>   I hear you singing on the leafless hills,
> And all my heart with jubilation thrills!
> You bring to me no message of dismay,
> No tender sorrow for the year's decay;
>   Rather you sing of giant trees that cast

Their leaves aside to grapple with the blast,
Strong and exultant for the stormy fray!

Hearing your music, glad and wild and pure,
   Sounding through night's cool, starlit spaces wide,
I grow aweary of earth's paltry lure!
   Oh, like the trees, I too would cast aside
   The fading leaves of pleasure and of pride,
And stand forth free to struggle and endure!

With this poem lodged in *Harper's,* one of the nation's most prestigious literary journals, Effie Waller Smith quit her serious writing effort. Why did she stop writing and publishing at the age of thirty-eight? Perhaps the writing process had become very painful for her, and certainly, the subjects and themes in nearly all of her later pieces indicate this most profoundly. Perhaps, for all her moderate publishing success, it was the publishing process itself that had become painful: the difficulty of getting her work read, recognized, and widely promulgated on a regular basis. Or perhaps the times were simply not right for a black woman writing several decades before the mainstream literary world was ready to celebrate such an effort. Indeed, it was not until 1950 that Gwendolyn Brooks became the first African-American woman to win the Pulitzer Prize for poetry. By that time, the singing poet of the Cumberlands had been silent for thirty-three years, and we can only speculate on the reasons why.

NOTES

1. "To Mary Elliott Flanery," in *Songs of the Months.*
2. Research indicates there are two extant copies of Waller's first book, *Songs of the Months,* published in 1904; approximately ten copies of her second book, *Rhymes from the Cumberland,* pub-

lished in 1909; and only three copies of her third book, *Rosemary and Pansies*, also published in 1909. In 1987 I republished these volumes in order to make her work more widely available. This second reprint in The Schomburg Library of Nineteenth-Century Black Women Writers should help to spread her writing even further.

3. *Marshall Wingfield, Wingfield's History of Caroline County* (N.p.: Regional Publishing Company, 1975), p. 483.

4. See the dedication in *Rosemary and Pansies* and the poem "My Brother" in the same volume. The poem gives Marvin's dates as 1882–1903, but there is some confusion over his existence. In the 1900 census, Sibbie reported that she bore three children and that three survived, yet in 1910 she reported that she bore four children and that three survived. My hypothesis is that Marvin was born with an affliction or deformity and that his family, ignorant of the causes of such, carried some burden of shame about it.

5. Interview with Ruth Smith, Neenah, Wisconsin, September 1987.

6. This school is now Kentucky State University.

7. Documentation for this cannot be located; school records for Greene County, Tennessee, were destroyed prior to an investigation on charges of nepotism.

8. According to Reverend J. J. Pipkin's book, *The History of a Rising Race: The Negro in Revelation, in History and in Citizenship* (N.p.: N. D. Thompson Publishing Co., 1902; rpt. Hallandale, Fla: New World Book Manufacturing Co., 1971), Waller published in the local papers of Pikeville and of Williamson, West Virginia.

9. In 1896 Mary Elliott Flanery moved to Pikeville from Boyd County, Kentucky, with her husband, W. Harvey Flanery, who went to work as an attorney for Northern Coal and Coke. Upon returning to Boyd County in 1911, she became involved in local politics and was elected to the state legislature in 1922, becoming the first woman south of the Mason–Dixon line to be elected to that position. During her one term in office, she devoted herself to working for women's suffrage and improved education. (author unknown) A short biographical sketch accompanies the papers of

Mary Elliott Flanery, held at the Margaret S. King Library, University of Kentucky.

10. Pipkin, *History of a Rising Race*.

11. Effie Waller's appearance in Pipkin's book was discovered when inquiry was made of her at the Moorland-Spingarn Research Center at Howard University in Washington, D.C. Luckily, work had been done there to index the names of African Americans who were mentioned prominently in certain works. The Moorland-Spingarn does not hold any copies of her books.

12. Ann Allen Shockley, *Afro-American Women Writers 1746–1933: An Anthology and Critical Guide* (Boston, MA: G. K. Hall, 1988). Upon reviewing my research, Shockley has indicated that she would now also include Waller's third book, *Rosemary and Pansies*, in her anthology.

13. It was a common practice to distribute volumes of an aspiring author's work in an effort to publicize them. This was the method employed by Dunbar's patrons who managed to place one of his books in the hands of William Dean Howells, who greatly advanced Dunbar's career by favorably reviewing the book in *Harper's Weekly* in 1896. However, no critical response to *Songs* can be documented.

14. Around 1911 or 1912. Interview with Amanda Roosevelt Owens Lark, Pikeville, Kentucky, September 1987.

15. The penultimate two poems of Part I describe a trip to an area of the Breaks so remote and difficult to reach as to require a guide, almost certainly a white mountaineer. In September 1987 I visited the Chimney Rocks, the place Waller speaks of in these poems. The going was very rough and my companion and I stayed lost until finally blundering into the Chimney Rocks in this very rugged area of the Breaks.

16. In her poem "At Pool Point," Waller refers to a boardinghouse in Elkhorn City, Kentucky, where she stayed on at least one of her visits to the Breaks. Jesse Stewart, former long-time resident of Elkhorn City, who now lives in Grundy, Virginia, holds one of the ten extant copies of *Rhymes*. In an interview in October 1988, he told me how his mother, Vicey Stewart, had been given her copy of *Rhymes* personally. Vicey, who lived in the Breaks at the time,

told him that she was one of the few white people who would talk to Effie as she made her way on foot into the Breaks to explore and write. Effie told Vicey that she was cooking for her board at a roominghouse for loggers in Elkhorn City. She also said that when her poems were printed she would bring Vicey a copy. Jesse Stewart thinks that it was in 1912 that Waller returned and repaid his mother's simple kindness with a copy of her book.

17. Several local interviews verify this.

18. Interview with Ron Bailey, chairman of Afro-American Studies Department at Northeastern University, Boston, May 1987.

19. The paper was scanned from 1885 through 1920.

20. Brown did not know Auxier's source for this information. It could well have come from Auxier's mother-in-law who held Waller's first two books. Both Auxier and her mother-in-law have long since died, leaving this particular question unanswerable.

21. See the discussion by John Michael Vlach in his book *The Afro-American Tradition in Decorative Arts* (Cleveland: The Cleveland Museum of Art [distributed by the Kent State University Press], 1978), pp. 139–43. In searching old graveyards around my home in Pikeville, two graves (c. 1900) of African Americans were found so decorated.

SHORT STORIES

☙ ☙ ☙

THE TEMPTING OF
PETER STILES

To be the black sheep of a respectable flock is not the worst fate. If one has good blood in one's veins, it may sometime assert itself, in spite of one's individual misdoing; but to be the ignoble scion of a long and worthless ancestry has an element of hopelessness in it.

Peter Stiles simply ran in the ruts which the generations before him had furrowed. His forefathers had handed down to him, together with pale eyes, sandy hair, butter-colored whiskers and insignificant features, their own utter shiftlessness and instability of character. Never was a man's name more unsuited to his nature, for in Peter Stiles's personality there was nothing remotely suggestive of a rock. Instead, his character seemed built on the most sliding, shifting, uncertain variety of sand imaginable, a structure which needed not to wait till the rain descended and the floods came, in order to fall but which might be expected to topple in the most trifling gust; which, indeed, if left alone, would probably have tumbled down of its own accord, simply because it was the most natural thing to do. At least that was what Deacon Gregg thought, and the Deacon was Peter Stiles's nearest neighbor, and therefore ought to know.

Just as Peter's instability made his Christian character the perpetual victim of circumstances and temptation, so it blocked the way to his becoming a consistent and successful sinner.

Putnam's Monthly 3 (Feb. 1908): 597–602.

Though he could not help straying from the fold, he bleated piteously when he was no longer in sight of it. Thus he was ever a subject for reviving grace, and the reclaiming of Peter Stiles came to be a regular feature of revivals in Long Hollow. If they that turn others to righteousness wear added jewels in their crown of light, surely Peter Stiles must have lent a sparkle to many a glorified brow.

For a month after one of these reconversions Peter would be the most ardent member of Long Hollow church, praying in public and giving the brethren and sisters the full benefit of his religious experience; during the second month he grew perceptibly colder; and at the end of the third month he was again a wandering sheep. Thus, if the removal occurred in mid-winter, Deacon Gregg was locking his spring-house as vigilantly as ever by the time the earliest spring cheese was made; and if it took place in summer he was prepared, as of old, to guard his favorite Winesap apples as they grew ripe in the late autumn.

For a long time Deacon Gregg had regarded Peter Stiles's cabin, perched on the hillside beyond the Deacon's meadow, as a sinister blot on the landscape. In its neighborhood strange things happened. If the Deacon's white turkey had chanced to make her nest in the meadow near it, she rarely brought home a brood; if an unusually fine pumpkin in the cornfield adjoining its confines had been reserved for seed, the fated vegetable mysteriously disappeared.

Yet in the appearance of the house, at least, there was nothing peculiar or enigmatic. It was not much more nor much less tumble-down than the ordinary cabin of the Tennessee mountains. There was the usual weed-flecked stick-and-clay chimney; the usual swayed and decaying roof; there were the usual pigmy windows on each side of the low door-windows which, having their original glass crusted with dirt or superseded by various cast-off garments, gazed with bleared and disconsolate vision across the mountain landscape. Before the door there was also the usual rail fence, from which dangled the usual bevy of tow-headed children.

This fence was continued in straggling and dilapidated panels around Peter Stiles's meagre farm. True, it hardly seemed necessary, for no animal, unless it were one of unusually poor judgment indeed, could have been tempted to trespass by the product of Peter Stiles's acres. His own stock he turned out on the common, where, left to their own resources, they speedily developed the ingenuity and address usually displayed by human beings in similar circumstances. There was, in particular, one ill-favored old sow whose skill and enterprise made her a character long remembered by the farmers of Long Hollow. Her appearance as she trotted jerkily along, the malignant countenance darkened by long, pendulous ears, the shadowy form not changed to the faintest suggestion of rotundity by all the crops she had destroyed, was not prepossessing; yet if you saw her at the head of a body of gaunt pigs, raiding cornfields, assaulting apparently impregnable fences, making forced marches to points of vantage, and eluding her canine pursuers by dexterous flank movements, you would have been obliged to admit that she was an expert tactician, and a genius in her way. The fact that her invasions were generally made into Deacon Gregg's territory did not tend to lessen the breach between the Deacon and her owner.

Deacon Gregg was an elderly man of portly presence and patriarchal beard, who wore the complacent air of one who has laid up treasures both in heaven and on earth. In the present world he had a good farm and a surplus in the county bank; with regard to the next world he was doubtless as well off; for no one could help perceiving that he had the indescribable severity of utterance and sanctity of mien proper to those who are better than most of their neighbors. On meeting days, his majestic form, walking slowly down the aisle to his accustomed seat in the Amen corner, was in itself impressive; and if by chance he read a Scripture lesson before the congregation, his tone and manner proclaimed more vehemently than the words of the Book, " 'The way of the transgressor is hard'—and it ought to be!"

To Peter Stiles he was especially severe. More than once his motion to turn Peter out of the church had been checkmated only by the penitent tears of the delinquent; and sometimes, when the brethren and sisters had shaken hands together in token of Christian fellowship, the Deacon had stood with a far-away look in his eyes, strangely oblivious of Peter Stiles's outstretched member.

One winter, just as the grudge between Peter and the Deacon had reached its climax, and they had ceased to have dealings together, or to speak to each other when they met, a revival meeting began in Long Hollow. The preacher was a young man, a stranger, whom the half admiring sinners described as "a hustler who was tearin' up the patch"; while the church members spoke of him as "a chosen vessel, who was shakin' the powers of the kingdom of darkness." He had a lean, sun-burnt countenance and a loose, ungainly figure; his awkward gait and toil-hardened hands spoke of a youth spent behind the plow; yet there was a fervid zeal smouldering in his dark eyes, and something in his half-ascetic face which thrilled his listeners with awe. When he brought his fist thundering down on the trembling desk, to emphasize his passionate pleading, when he shook the opened Book terrifyingly in the faces of those whom its words should one day judge, the audience felt that behind vehement speech and violent gesture was the preacher's absolute conviction that what he said was true. Before that absolute conviction the sinners of Long Hollow wilted; and Peter Stiles found himself frantically resolving that if ever he got religion again he would hang on to it.

It was a wonderful meeting. For years afterward the devout ones of Long Hollow spoke of it as "a time of great out-pourin' in Zion." But though, as the days passed, many a hardened sinner was melted, many a cold church member warmed, Peter Stiles still sat in a dark corner with dejected figure and disconsolate eyes, his whole soul seemingly numbed with the apathy of despair. Old brethren, who had been disgusted with his inconsistencies, now became really solicitous about one who, they feared, had grieved the Spirit beyond recalling. Jim Madden, an untamable sinner who had not seldom borne Peter company in the paths of unrighteousness, said that, as often as Peter had got religion, he ought to know how by that time, and not find it such a hard job.

The last day of the meeting arrived; the last sermon was preached, the last prayer offered, and the shadow of hopelessness that shrouded Peter Stiles's soul grew black. At the close of the prayer the preacher asked that all the Christians present, especially those who in time past had not been living in peace and harmony, should come forward to the open space before the pulpit, and clasp one another's hands in brotherly love and reconciliation.

This peacemaking among church members was the inevitable winding-up of a Long Hollow revival. Anyone who had "stood out" a revival without making up with those who had a grudge against him, would have been considered hard-hearted indeed. Unfortunately, the peace thus established was generally broken within a few weeks after the meeting closed, and the estranged brethren or sisters were obliged to wait till the next revival to effect another reconciliation. In this way, petty squabble and spasmodic truce succeeded each other, till at length both were merged in the enduring peace of death.

At the preacher's invitation there was a general scramble to the designated spot. Mrs. Hornby's fat brown palm tremblingly squeezed the slim, claw-like hand of the widow Bates, whose geese had once invaded Mrs. Hornby's garden, to the great detriment of both ladies' Christian character, and the utter demolishing of the vegetables. The checked sun-bonnet of Mrs. Cleever, whose son Amos's unrequited affection for Miss Milly Burnley had been the beginning of a long series of accusations and recriminations between the mothers of the young people, shook in convulsive reconciliation as it met the antiquated toque of Mrs. Burnley. Squire Sims and Captain Biddle, who had not spoken to each other since the Presidential campaign two years before, now laid aside the discordant memories of election day. Just as the hand-shaking began to subside, a drooping figure raised itself from the mourners' bench, and Peter Stiles's limp hand was held out feebly toward the rest. Among those who seized and clasped it was Deacon Gregg.

In the weeks succeeding the revival, Peter Stiles did not display his usual spiritual fluency. Never before had he made a less imposing exhibition of the religion he had recently acquired. True, he went to preaching and to prayer-meeting with clock-like regularity; but it was only on rare occasions that he could be brought to indulge even in a devout groan or a reverberating Amen. Jim Madden said that Peter, having had so much trouble in getting religion this time, did not want to use it up all at once, but, by being economical, hoped to spin it out a long way.

Winter budded into spring, and spring blossomed brilliantly into summer, but Deacon Gregg's cherries ripened unmolested save by the sparrows, and Deacon Gregg's early

chickens advanced to frying size under the shadow of no
greater menace than that of the hawks. When the end of
August approached, and Peter Stiles's usually slippery feet
had not yet slidden from the straight and narrow path, Long
Hollow began to wonder. Jim Madden was especially puz-
zled, and when his own ingenuity, assisted by the surmises
of half a dozen neighbors, had failed to satisfy him, he
resolved to make a tour of investigation and bring the matter
to a test.

It was after sunset of an August day, and Peter Stiles was
sitting on the fence before his door, resting from his day's
work. A horse's footstep sounded on the rocky road, and Jim
Madden ambled up in the most casual manner in the world.
Naturally he drew rein to give his friend the usual salutation,
"Howdy, Peter. Lordy, ain't it hot?"

Peter returned the greeting, and there followed an elaborate
discussion of the likelihood or unlikelihood of rain—a discussion which never loses its freshness to those who win their
living from the soil, but which is especially interesting at
those seasons when rain and topics of conversation are alike
scarce.

A pensive look came into Jim Madden's eyes. "La, Peter,
how good a water-million would taste now! I planted my
patch too late, I 'low, and it's plum burnt up. I reckon you've
had 'em till you're tired out on 'em."

Peter replied with a slow shake of his head. "I ha' n't
tasted a water-million this year. I didn't plant none, for I
knowed it was no use: they never do no good for me nohow."

Jim Madden's eyes widened with well-feigned surprise.
"Somebody was tellin' me that Deacon Gregg had a mighty
fine patch, but I 'low it was a mistake. A body can hear most
anything these days."

"They say, for certain, that the Deacon has got some purty

ones; but," added Peter, "Deacon Gregg's water-millions don't belong to me."

The emphasis with which Peter uttered this self-evident truth brought a shade of righteous indignation to his companion's face. "Lordy, that's so. I ought to 'a' knowed them millions would n't 'a' benefited you any. The Deacon wouldn't give you the measles if he had 'em, he's so sot agin givin' a body anything."

The shadow faded from Jim Madden's countenance, and an inscrutable smile took its place. He nodded his head with such an air of mysterious significance as could not fail to impress the attentive Peter. Then he bent down, and, in the confidential tone which Peter so well remembered, he murmured: "I tell you it's a sin to let them water-millions rot in the patch! Me and you could save two or three of them from that distressin' fate this very night, and nobody would be a mite sadder nor wiser."

Peter's half-raised arm was suggestive of the entreaty, "Get thee behind me, Satan," but slowly the arm subsided, and his companion went on: "The Deacon turns his big dog loose every night, but I can work that satisfactory to all parties. Along after dark awhile, I'll happen in at the Deacon's to borrow his big plow. While the dogs is a-ravin' and the Deacon receivin' me—"

"You can't git the plow, Jim," Peter interrupted; "the Deacon won't lend to nobody."

Jim Madden laughed uproariously. "I don't want no plow, you goose; all I want is to git the Deacon and the dogs to entertain me at the front gate while you creep over the back palin's. While I'm a pleadin' pitiful for the plow, and the Deacon is mindin' off the dogs and lecturin' me on my shiftlessness, you pick us out some purty millions an streak towards home. You can cross over into the lane at that big walnut tree, and when ye get to the woods, set down and wait till I ketch up. You eat your supper and then keep your ears open, and after a while, when you hear the dogs a-barkin' furious down at the Deacon's, jest pick ye up a sack and light out for the water-million patch."

Peter shook his head gravely. "I'd ruther not, Jim," he said. "Me and the Deacon's friendly now, and he might find out about the millions, and we'd fuss again. I'd ruther not, Jim."

Only an old companion in iniquity could have detected the note of indecision in Peter Stiles's grunt of dissent; but Jim Madden chuckled when he got out of hearing. If Peter's religion should be weighed in the balance with a big water-melon, Jim felt reasonably sure that the melon would not be found wanting.

For several minutes after his tempter had gone Peter Stiles sat in a deep study. From generation to generation of the Stiles family the tradition had been handed down that the eighth commandment did not apply to water-melons. Peter's mind was now agitated by a wild conflict between the commandment and this tradition of the elders. At length he dismounted the fence and walked slowly to the barn, from which he soon emerged, carrying a large empty meal bag. This he slung in a convenient corner of the fence, and then, grave and silent, he entered the cabin and took his place at the table, whereon the scant supper was spread.

Twilight had deepened into dusk, when, supper ended, he sat down in the doorway, where the mountain breeze might fan his hot cheek. The rising moon was beginning to transform the rugged landscape into a loveliness surpassing that of dreams. All around, the great hills, rising serene above human strife, standing firm amidst human instability, seemed to look down with majestic pity and silent reproachfulness.

In the deep stillness, the roar of the far-off river was audible, the echoes of sheep-bells, and the faint music of distant voices singing. Suddenly, drowning all other sounds, sharp, clear and loud, rose the fierce barking of the Deacon's dogs.

Peter got up as unconcernedly as possible, and reached for his hat. "I'll be back agin bed-time," he promised his wife, as he went out. Taking the meal bag from its hiding-place, he wound it into a tight roll, to make it as small as possible, and tucked it under his arm; then he leaped the fence and entered the strip of woodland which separated his cabin from Deacon Gregg's meadow.

As he walked along the shadowy road, his steps were halting and reluctant. "I wish to goodness," he muttered, "that I'd 'a' let Jim have my end of the bargain. He's a heap keener for water-millions than I am, comin' this early. But the Deacon don't need so many millions, nohow."

His hesitation ceased when he emerged from the woods. Before him the Deacon's meadow, wide and smooth compared with the other meadows of Long Hollow, lay still and fair in the white moonlight. At the other end of it stood the Deacon's house; and near the house, well enclosed by a picket fence, was the water-melon patch. Peter could see its foliage gleaming in contrast with the paler hue of the meadow grass.

Entering the lane that led to the house, he walked swiftly in the shadow of the fence. A few yards from his destination he paused beneath a huge walnut tree, and crossing the fence crept through the tall grass till he reached the picketed enclosure. Then he stood still and listened; the dogs were still barking furiously, and above their din he could hear the Deacon's voice raised in angry expostulation. With the dexterity born of long practice, Peter Stiles swung himself over the fence, down to the ground, where the Deacon's melons wee shining amid the dewy leaves.

If Peter had not been so intent on his task he might have heard the terrified squealing of pigs. When Deacon Gregg had gone out to give his hogs their night feed, he had found his own herd accompanied, as usual, by Peter Stiles's. The Deacon was a firm believer in close communion; Peter Stiles's hogs did not agree with him. When the hogs remained steadfast in their opinion, and proceeded to act on it vigorously, the Deacon called out his dogs to help refute the dissenters. It was against Peter's hogs, therefore, and not against Jim Madden, that the loud clamor of the dogs was directed. The heretics were put to confusion, and even the fierce old sow was brought to bay. When the Deacon had restored peace, and had got the dogs into the yard again, one ill-starred pig lay in the fencer corner, never more to thrust its lean nose into forbidden troughs.

Deacon Gregg was troubled. He knew Peter well enough to feel sure that he would be furious at the killing of the pig, and, if the Deacon did not make the loss good, would doubtless take the matter to law, and collect damages, if possible. Even if he did not succeed in this, there would be hard feelings and reprisals which the Deacon dreaded to encounter. He reasoned that it would be against the best interests of the church, and hurtful to the spiritual welfare of Peter Stiles, to stir up needless strife by allowing it to be known how the pig had met its fate. The Book had said quite plainly that no man ought to put a stumbling-block or an occasion to fall in his brother's way. He decided to carry the pig off, and throw it far into the shade of the woods, where, if Peter ever found it, he could have no proof of who was its slayer. Dispersing the bereaved sow and pigs, now gathered round their fallen kinsman, grunting ominous threats of vengeance, the Deacon lifted the pig and started with it up the lane.

When Peter Stiles, returning with a huge melon in each end of the bag, was crossing the fence into the lane, he heard footsteps approaching. From behind the walnut tree, he stepped out into the moonlight to meet Jim and assure him that all was well; but ws thunder-struck to find himself face to face with Deacon Gregg.

Both men stopped, recoiled, and for a few seconds stood silent, returning each other's startled gaze. Peter's face had blazed with sudden anger at the sight of Deacon Gregg's burden; but before he could speak, the thought of the Deacon's stolen melons on his shoulder made his fury helpless. The Deacon had gasped in virtuous indignation, yet he realized that with Peter's mangled pig in his hands it was impossible to attempt a moral lecture. But he recovered first, and faced the situation.

"Good evenin', Peter," he said, in his bland, imposing, prayer-meeting tones. "I'm sorry to say that my fierce dogs have accidentally killed one of your pigs. I jest started up to ask you the damage."

Peter caught his breath; but a moment later he answered in a voice of perfect meekness: "Nothin' at all, I reckon, Deacon. My hogs has pestered you a heap, off and on, and I 'low that killin' 's the best thing you could do for 'em."

Then in his most matter-of-fact way he added: "I 'lowed you had so many water-millions, Deacon, that you could n't make use of 'em all, so I come down to fetch one or two to the children. I didn't think to ax you, but I didn't 'low you'd mind."

If Deacon Gregg's business all his life had been only to give away water-melons, he could not have answered with a more accomplished and magnanimous grace. "That's all right, Peter. I'm powerful glad you got 'em. They's so many of 'em, they 're spilin' in the patch, and ruinin' the vines."

An hour later, when Peter Stiles was in bed, and all that remained of the melons was a big mound of gnawed-out rinds in the back yard, Jim Madden came to the entrance of the lane, ostensibly on his way to borrow the Deacon's plow. At the edge of the woods he stopped, and gave a long, cautious whistle. When he had listened in vain for a response, he softly called Peter's name; then he looked anxiously over the meadow and waited; but meadow and woodland alike remained hushed and motionless. After a quarter of an hour he bent his steps toward Peter Stiles's cabin. The door was closed, the windows were dark; if any creature on the place was awake there was no evidence of the fact.

Jim Madden gave a low ejaculation of wonder as he turned homeward. "I'll be ducked," said he, "if Pete Stiles ha'n't got religion after all!"

A SON OF SORROW

On that unforgettable Sunday night, Narcissy McClure and her lover did not say goodby. The quarrel between them had been bitter, and as they parted there were no softening words uttered. At the gate George Wisterne turned abruptly away, and Narcissy passed haughtily up the path to the cabin door.

As the girl stepped into the firelit room, her mother looked up in startled questioning. Her father, laboriously spelling out a chapter in the huge Bible, let his heavy forefinger slip from its place.

"What 's the matter, Narcissy, and whar 's George?"

"Thar ain't nothin' the matter," she answered resolutely, though her voice trembled. "Me and George has hed a split-up, and we've quit fer good and all!"

The shocked silence that followed was broken by the old woman. "How come you-uns to fall out?"

"As we come from the singin' to-night, George told me that him and Sylvester Flanary hed laid off to put up a store and go in together a-sellin' goods. Sylvester's aimin' to do most of the tradin', so 's George kin keep on with the lumber business at the same time. George was powerful took with the idea. But when he axed me how I liked it, I told him what a bad name Sylvester has allus bore in these parts, and how folks wouldn't think nothin' of him ef he took up with sich a feller. We hed a tear-up then, and before I knowed it, I 'd said straight out that nobody should keep company with me, that was a pardner of Sylvester Flanary's. 'All right, ef

Putnam's and the Reader 5 (Dec. 1908): 274–80.

you 're that onreasonable!' George says. Atter that, nary one of us spoke another word."

At the mention of Sylvester Flanary's name, Narcissy's father shook his head ominously, and her mother's face grew hard. Sylvester was known on Pine Ridge and in all the neighboring country as a shaky character. Dark stories were told concerning transactions in which he had been engaged, and still darker suspicions were hinted of deeds which had never been definitely proved. Yet he had managed to escape the clutches of the law; and a plausible way he had, together with his dexterity in business, gave him a certain hold on people.

"It's a mighty quair notion, goin' in cahoot with a feller like that!" the old man muttered. "Still, George hain't been here long, and mebbe he don't known as much about Sylvester Flanary as the balance of us does."

"Ef George don't know Sylvester, he 's got plenty o' chances to find out about him! 'Birds of a feather flock together,' *I 've* allus heerd," Mrs. McClure quoted dismally. "But, Narcissy, I 'low you spoke up too peert with George, and got him riled. Ef you 'd sorter hinted what you thought, 'stid o' tellin' him plain out, mebbe he 'd 'a' listened to you."

"Don't you git pestered about it, Narcissy," said her father. "Ef George Wisterne is the right kind, he'll find Sylvester out, some day; and ef he 's Sylvester Flanary's kind, you 're pow'ful lucky to git shet of him."

"Mebbe it 's fer the best, atter all," admitted the old woman, her grim face relaxing a ltitle. "It ain't like it 'ud be ef you didn't hev no other beaus. Now, ef you and Benoni—"

"Benoni! Don't say nary word about Benoni to me!" With an impatient gesture, the girl turned and sped up the narrow stairs to her own room.

"That 's the way of her!" complained Mrs McClure. "Jest mention Benoni Harwood's name, and she 's gone like a streak o' lightnin'. Well, gals is quair! Ef a feller lives close by 'em and is allus good to 'em, they won't look at him; but let some dressed-up stranger come along, and they 're plumb carried away."

On her road from church, a few weeks afterward, Narcissy was overtaken by Benoni Harwood. He did not, in his frank joy at seeing her, appear to notice how silent she was. At the parting of their ways, he looked at her appealingly.

"Could I come up awhile this evenin', Narcissy? That is, ef you ain't expectin' nobody else."

"Thar won't be nobody else, but I'd ruther you wouldn't come, Benoni," she answered firmly.

If anyone except Benoni had asked to spend the evening with her, Narcissy would gladly have assented. Nothing could have pleased her better just then than to have a new "beau"—"to carry on with a feller that didn't mean nothin',—" and thus to show George Wisterne that there were other men besides himself whom she could enjoy talking to. But she dared not use Benoni Harwood for that purpose. The dead earnestness of his lvove for her made her afraid; and when he looked at her with his wide, wistful eyes she was troubled.

"Benoni takes them big, lonesome eyes atter his mammy," Aunt Hephzibah Landers used to say. "She warn't raised in the mountains, Mis' Harwood warn't. She come from Virginny or some'rs—run off and got married to Jeems Harwood when he was up thar buyin' hosses fer old 'Squire Towson. Jeems warn't no manner of account, but he was pow'ful good-lookin', and hed a mighty takin' way with gals. She never got used to the mountains—allus hed a fur-off, homesick look in her eyes, jest like Benoni's got."

Whatever grief or loneliness Jeems Harwood's wife had endured, she had kept to herself. Only one token had she given of her life's disappointment. When her boy was born, in the bitterness of her soul she had named him Benoni— "Son of My Sorrow."

She had died so early that he hardly remembered her. "Benoni never took to his pappy much," and after that terrible day when the saw-log slipped and rolled down on the man, crushing out his worthless life, the boy, though shocked and grieved beyond measure, was hardly more lonely than before.

At his father's death, kindly Mrs. McClure had taken Benoni to her heart, and insisted that for a time he should make his home with her. It was in those days that he had begun to love his merry-hearted little playmate. His love for Narcissy had deepened as the years passed. In the long days when he plowed and hoed his crop on the stony hills, his hope of working for her and not for himself alone, strengthened his hands; and returning at nightfall to his lonely cabin, he forgot its emptiness in thinking that Narcissy would some day come to be with him there.

It was different with her. If she thought at all of their childish love-making, she regarded it merely as a part of their play. When finally he had told her of his long-cherished hope, she had met him with a firm refusal.

"What ever put sich a notion in your head, Benoni? O' course, we used to play sweethearts when we was little-uns, but thar warn't nothin' in that, no more 'n in blindfold or whoop-hide!"

"I can't believe but what you 'll be mind some time, Narcissy," he had answered gravely. "I kin wait years and years fer you to change your mind, but as long as we live and you ain't married to some other feller, I won't give you up!"

Narcissy had done her best to discourage this attitude. There seemed something ominous and oppressive in Benoni's silent longing and unwearied waiting.

The new store opened with unusual promise. Sylvester Flanary was a most affable salesman, and, though the partners had had only a few hundred dollars to invest, the stock was so carefully selected and so skilfully displayed that it seemed very imposing indeed to a community whose wants were as few as those of Pine Ridge.

In the general admiration aroused by the new merchants' success, Narcissy's scruples received little sympathy. More than one old woman remarked meaningly that Narcissy McClure would know better next time than to turn off such a nice young man just for a fool notion. "Folks don't need to be so pertickler, nohow. Lots of gals is like butterflies—they 'll fly high all day and light on the ground at night!" Down in her heart, the girl shared these misgivings. She told herself resolutely that she did not want George Wisterne or any other man unless she knew he ws fair and square; yet all through the long summer and the laggard autumn, she found herself wondering if she had not been too hasty in sending her lover away.

Mrs. McClure was hardly less perplexed and grieved than Narcissy. Her dearest hope had been that she might live to see all her large family of girls married and settled in homes of their own. Her other daughters, not being so pretty as Narcissy, and consequently having fewer lovers to select from, had not wasted much time in making a choice; and they had successively gone out from the parental cabin to take their places in sundry other cabins scattered among the neighboring coves and ridges.

"The rest of 'em has done well enough," the old woman

would mutter, "all but Narcissy, and her the takin'est gal
I 've got! 'Pears like them that the Lord gives most to, a
heap o' times makes the least use of it. Narcissy ain't nary bit
nigher marryin' now than she was two years ago. I wish to
goodness George Wisterne hed never set foot on Pine Ridge,
so 's she might 'a' hed eyes fer somebody else!"

Once or twice Narcissy had met George at the store, and
they had greeted each other with distant politeness. But she
did not often go there, so distasteful was the place to her.
Thus, when, late in December, the "Christmas fixin's" were
to be bought, she delegated to her father even that important
task.

It was dark when the old man reached home. "Thar,
Narcissy," he said, laying an armful of packages on the
kitchen table, "thar 's all of your tricks I could git. They was
out of several things you wanted."

Narcissy looked up in surprise. "I thought they allus kept
sich a full stock, and never run out o' nothin'."

" 'Pears like they hev got a full stock. The store's crammed
so, you can't hardly turn around. And yit," the old man's
shrewd eyes clouded, "I 've got my doubts about what 's in
all them boxes and bar'ls."

"What d' ye mean by sayin' that?"

"I 'll tell you what I seed myself. A man come this evenin'
to buy a pair of shoes. Sylvester 'd gone over to Rocky P'int
to see his brother's child that's got dipthery, and George hed
to do the tradin'. The shelves was full of shoe-boxes, and he
handed one down; but when he opened it, the box was plumb
empty! George turned red, and he peeped in another box or
two, that he didn't take down. Then he went acrost the store
and hunted till he found some shoes, and sold the man a pair.
But I'll bet thar warn't nothin' in all them boxes he fust went
to!"

"That's jest puttin' on," declared Narcissy, scornfully.

"Course it is, honey. They want to make out like they've got a heap o' goods, bekase folks'll buy quicker from a feller when they think he 's runnin' a big business."

"It looks like George ort to keep better posted about his own store, and not be openin' the empty boxes before folks," Mrs. McClure interposed, sarcastically.

"George hain't been in the store much lately. He 's been sawin' lumber over on Mill Creek, and he ain't quite up to waitin' on folks. W'y, when Benoni Harwood axed to settle up his accounts, George couldn't even find the account-books—looked everywhar fer 'em, and at last told Benoni he 'd hev to come back when Sylvester was thar, fer the books warn't in the place they used to keep 'em."

While this conversation was taking place, George Wisterne, left alone at the store, was going around, peering into various bags and cases. He frowned heavily as he finished a cursory examination of the stock.

"Sylvester 's shorely let the goods run mighty low, 'specially fer Christmas time," he muttered. "We 'll be losin' trade d'rectly, ef we can't keep things up no better 'n this. I 'll speak to him about it, soon 's he comes home. We 'll overhaul them shelves too, and straighten up a little, ef I 've got any say-so about it," he added, as his glance fell darkly on the rows of empty boxes.

Nothing could be done to-night, however; so, locking the door behind him, he went a few yards down the road to Sylvester Flanary's, where he boarded. After supper, he found the missing account-books lying on Sylvester's desk. Taking them up, he busied himself with their contents till bedtime.

From a sound sleep he was awakened by Mrs. Flanary's

trembling voice outside his door. "O Mr. Wisterne," she pleaded, "do go out and see ef thar 's anything wrong at the store! Sylvester hain't come back and I 'm shore I heerd a noise jest now."

Two minutes later, George had started to find out the cause of Mrs. Flanary's alarm. Suddenly every window of the store shone dazzlingly out as a blaze swept through the entire building. At the same instant rose the tumultuous sound of flames.

Shouting to Mrs. Flanary that she must wake the children and send them for help, the young man hurried to the fire. But even before he reached it, he realized that nothing could save the store.

The building had long been a heap of embers when, an hour after sunrise, Sylvester Flanary reached home. He seemed much shocked on learning of the fire, but gave a ready explanation of how it might have occurred.

"You say, George, that the blaze started on the inside? Well, then it 's plain enough how it was. Not bein' used to shuttin' up, you 've been a leetle keerless about the fire in the stove, and sometin' 's cotch from it. But I ain't a-blamin' you. Accidents will happen."

"I can't think it started that way," George maintained stoutly. "The fire was mighty nigh out when I left, and I made shore thar warn't no danger from it."

"Mebbe the mice got to gnawin' in the matches, then, and sot 'em afire. We ain't apt ever to find out jest how it happened, bekase nobody seed it."

The news spread rapidly, and during the day nearly every man and boy on Pine Ridge visited the scene of the fire.

It was not long before George noticed something singular in the manner of these visitors. If he approached several men talking earnestly together, a sudden hush would fall upon the group; and at times he fancied he was watched by curious and unfriendly eyes.

"You fellers seem to be enjoyin' yourselves," he remarked pleasantly, as he came up to a laughing crowd.

"I 'low you 're the one that 's enjoyin' yourself," a bold-faced young man spoke up. "How much will you git from the insurance company—twenty-five hundred dollars? That 'll set you and Sylvester up purty well, won't it?"

The insolence with which the words were uttered, and the loud guffaw that greeted them, revealed to George Wisterne exactly how he stood. He knew now the suspicions that had been whispered around him. His face paled and his hands clenched.

"I'd like fer you to explain what you mean by that," he said in a low voice.

"Thar ain't nothin' to explain," sneered the other. "I jest meant what I said. Insurance is a mighty handy thing, fer accidents will happen, you know."

George did not reply. He recognized the futility of any word he could say. The men had already made up their minds as to his guilt.

All day, George Wisterne's trial for the burning of the store had gone on at the tribunal of his neighbors' opinion. The separate links of circumstantial evidence had been woven into a chain which, while it might not have held in a court of law, seemed amply strong to the men of Pine Ridge. The facts that the store was heavily insured, and that the stock of goods had been allowed to run so low that the actual loss was comparatively small, took on a double significance when told in connection with the unexplained removal of the account-books on the day before the fire. Back of all, intensifying every suspicion, was the evil reputation that Sylvester Flanary had so long borne.

The suspicion of mountaineers is no light matter. There is something terrible in its fixedness. George knew that nothing short of a demonstration of his innocence could set him right in people's esteem.

"What on earth makes you look so down in the mouth, George?" asked Sylvester Flanary, when at nightfall the two men sat alone. "Thar ain't nary bit o' call to lose heart. When we git our insurance money, we 'll be able to start out on a right smart better footin' than we did afore."

George lifted his miserable eyes to his partner's face. "Do you know what people is sayin' about us—'bout us and the insurance money?"

"I don't keer a snap o' my finger what they say! They 'll be quick enough to trade with us when we git our new buildin' up, and a new stock o' goods laid in. And ef folks trades with us, they kin talk what they please behind our back!"

"I don't feel that way. What people says pesters me."

"Look here, George!" Sylvester spoke fiercely, "ef you sot that store afire, it's your privilege to go out and tell everybody you meet. I hain't got no confessions to make, myself. Nobody kin lay it to me, fer I kin prove that I didn't leave Rocky P'int till seven o'clock this mornin'. Now, onless you want folks to think you done it, you better not go round lookin' like a sheep-killin' dog."

"I wish to goodness I could take it as easy as you do. Fer my part, I 'd give a right smart to git things all straightened out."

"Things'll straighten their selves out atter while, ef you jest let 'em alone," Sylvester assured him.

For a long time after his partner had retired, George Wisterne sat gazing abstractedly into the fire. Involuntarily his thoughts went back to his last walk with Narcissy, and to her words concerning Sylvester Flanary—"Folks won't think nothin' of you ef you take up with sich a feller."

He wondered if she, like everybody else, would believe him guilty. His heart smote hiim as he realized that Narcissy's good opinion, which he had seemed to despise, meant more to him than he had ever guessed. A passionate desire to vindicate himself arose in him. Ah, if the truth about the fire could only be found out! But, as Sylvester Flanary had said, there were no witnesses.

Yet Sylvester was mistaken. There had been a witness, after all.

On leaving the store, the afternoon before it was burned, Benoni Harwood had gone across the ridge to get his wages from a farmer of the adjacent valley. He had been detained, and it was late in the night when, on his way home, he again passed the store.

As he came in sight, he saw a man cross the moon-lit road and enter the building. Thinking that, if Sylvester had returned, he might now have opportunity to transact the business that had brought him thither some hours earlier, Benoni went to the door. The store was dark, but he fancied he heard somebody moving around inside, and he caught the strong odor of kerosene. Just then there was the flash of a match, and a blinding flare.

As the incendiary sprang out and ran into the woods, he dashed heavily against Benoni, who had been too astonished to move. The young man recognized Jake Snyder, an ill-favored fellow who lived on Sylvester Flanary's place, and did odd jobs for him.

Benoni's first intention was to find some suitable person and tell what he had seen. But almost before he left his own doorway next morning, the report reached him that George Wisterne had burned the store in order to obtain the insurance money. After that, he held his peace.

Benoni was now meeting the deadliest temptation of his life. He had long known that George Wisterne stood between him and Narcissy. The suspicion George had incurred by becoming Flanary's partner, though it had clouded her love for him, had not destroyed it. If her confidence in him were restored, he could win her easily enough. On the other hand, Benoni felt sure that she would never marry George if she believed him guilty of burning the store. He held in his own hands the information which alone could clear his rival's name. If he chose to keep silence, Narcissy might yet be his.

All his life Benoni had tried in a vague way to do the right thing, and he had never had much trouble in finding out what the right thing was. The struggle he now underwent was therefore new and terrible to him.

At dusk he sought the mountains, and in their vast solitude he fought his battle over and over to the same futile conclusion. "She 's all I want, she 's all I 've ever wanted, and George Wisterne sha'n't hev her ef I kin hinder him!" he said a hundred times; but the words, so often and so fiercely repeated, did not satisfy him.

He paused as he reached the top of the ridge, and the wind that is forever stirring on the lonely summits smote him keenly in the face.

Far to the south, the peak of Chimney Top rose dark above the surrounding hills. In the loneliness of his youth, Benoni's spirit had been more than usually open to the influences of vastness and mystery held by the wild scenery around him. Now, when in the crisis of his struggle he looked upon it, the stern, immovable peak held for him a new significance. It seemed an image of the Will of God, unchangeable, inexorable, never to be turned aside by man's desire, nor satisfied by pretext or compromise. In an agony of renunciation, he flung out his arms toward the midnight sky and the infinite Being who, somewhere within it or beyond it, was looking down upon him. "O God," he cried aloud, "I can't hold out agin Ye no longer! You kin hev Your way!"

As he turned homeward, the moonlight, falling between the hemlock trees across his lifted face, showed it wan and worn, yet full of peace. Before sunrise next morning he was on his way to tell Wisterne all he knew about the burning of the store.

It was past noon on the third day after the fire, when Benoni opened the gate of the McClure homestead. He carried a valise, for he was leaving the mountains. Slowly and reluctantly he walked up the path. It was a hard task that he had set himself.

Narcissy rose half-frightened as he came in. "La, Benoni, thar ain't nothin' wrong, is thar?"

Benoni went straight to the purpose of his visit. "I hain't come over to-day bekase I wanted to, Narcissy. I 've come to tell you somethin' that nobody else kin tell as well as I kin, fer notbody else has seed all I've seed. You know folks has been sayin' hard things about George Wisterne. Well, folks is all wrong, and George hain't hed no more to do with burnin' that store than you hev!"

At the mention of her lover's name, the color had faded from Narcissy's face, and then flared back more brilliant than ever. She listened in palpitant silence as Benoni told how he had seen Snyder set fire to the store.

"George wanted me to go with him to git a warrant fer

Jake," he continued, "and we struck out to 'Squire Brinton's yistiddy mornin'. We didn't git back till jest a while ago, fer the 'Squire was tendin' a call meetin' of the County Court, and we hed to go plumb to town atter the warrant."

"Has Snyder been took up yit!"

"No, and he ain't apt to be. He 's gone—him and Sylvester both. I reckon Jake must 'a' seed who I was when he run agin me that night; and when me and George started to the 'Squire's, they knowed it was time fer 'em to move out."

"Can't nobody find out whar they went?"

"I 'm afeard not. George is keen to pop the law to 'em, fer he says he can't look you in the face till things is cleared up. But I 'low he nee'n't to pester hisself. Sylvester 's too old a bird to be cotch now."

Narcissy laughed happily. "I don't reckon it matters much whar Jake and Sylvester went, jest so George gits back his good name!"

"Well, he 'll git it back all right now, and—I wish you-uns both much joy, Narcissy!"

The young man's voice broke as he uttered the time-honored words of congratulation. A sudden, impulsive pity smote Narcissy, looking on his haggard face.

"I wish to God, Benoni," she faltered, "that I could 'a' loved you, or that you could 'a' loved some other gal!"

For one moment Benoni's anguish darkened his hungry eyes. His face worked with the effort to control his emotion; then he rose calmly and took up his valise.

"I reckon I 'd better be goin' on," he said, casually. "It 'll be gittin' late d'rectly, and I want to cross the mountain afore dark."

THE JUDGMENT
OF ROXENIE

"As the Almighty 's my witness, 'pears to me like you 're a-runnin' religion in the ground, a-settin' so much store by a passel of things that the Lord ain't no-wise pertickler about!"

It was the time of the annual Sacrament and crowds of people had gathered at the Dunkard meeting-house from every ridge and hollow for miles around. Even amid the unusual flutter of life and color that now invested it, the low log building, standing against the sombreness of innumerable pines that cover Bays Mountain, had a bleak and melancholy aspect. In its best days its appearance had not been cheerful, and time and storm had dealt with it hardly, darkening its walls to a sober brown, and seaming them with numberless fissures; here and there the mortar had fallen away from between the logs, leaving unsightly chinks and crannies; and several broken panes of the small window gave jagged glimpses of an austere and gloomy interior.

Under a huge buckeye tree near the meeting-house, three or four people, whose appearance was singularly in keeping with the scene around them, were engaged in earnest discussion. With one exception, they were old men, whose stern, deep-lined faces bore indelible records of the hardship of their long lives and the asceticism of their religion. According to Dunkard custom, they wore long hair; and the cut of

Putnam's Monthly 6 (June 1909): 309–17.

their beards, closely shaven except for a single gray tuft on the chin, gave an odd, half-monstrous aspect to their faces.

The young man who had just spoken differed from the rest of the group in more respects than his youth. True, his rich hair fell back from his forehead in long waves; and his dress was, like that of the others, rigidly plain even according to the mountain standards of simplicity. Yet his face, for all its seriousness, had a warmth, a suggested capacity for passion and struggle, which his companions had probably never known. As the Brethren put it, Ephraim Utsman looked like a man in whom the old Adam would die hard.

At his passionate words, a shocked murmur came from the listeners. "Who air we," a little fiery-eyed man broke in with shrill vehemence, "who are we to jedge what the Lord is pertickler about! When the Almighty lays His commands on us, what mortal man has got the right to say that ary word of 'em be left out?"

The protest which rose to Ephraim's lips was interrupted by a derisive laugh from one of the deacons. "Ephraim," he sneered, "is it bekase ye 've been keepin' company with Roxenie that yer tongue 's tied so 's you can't reprove her sins? It 's a evil day when a da'ter of the church gits took up with the onrighteous Mammon, and goes to puttin' on breast-pins and ruffles; and the wust part of it is, that him that the Brethren 's chose to guide their feet in the straight and narrer path, is upholdin' her in her folly. You 've got to take yer stand on one side or t' other, Ephraim! Ef in yer secret heart you 're a-puttin' Roxenie Pulliam afore the Lord's cause, yer sin 's a-goin' to find you out!"

"The Lord knows I ain't a-puttin' Roxenie afore His cause, Deacon Hunley," declared the young pastor, "but it ain't right and jest fer you-uns to be so set agin her. I don't say that she ha'n't got vain and foolish ways, but I 'low she don't mean no rale harm."

"Don't mean no harm!" Deacon Hunley echoed, scornfully. "Can't everybody see that the gal carries a high head and a proud look jest like her pappy and grandpappy did afore her?" The old man's brow darkened with sombre recollection. "I knowed her fore-payrents well enough, and I knowed 'em to my sorrer!"

The rich odor stealing from the meeting-house kitchen announced that the lamb to be used at the supper was now ready. As the men turned toward the low dooray, one of the deacons, whose age-bleached and sharpened features still bore a strong resemblance to Ephraim's own, laid a detaining hand on his arm.

"Be keerful, Ephe," warned the shaking voice, "be mighty keerful that you don't listen to the call o' flesh and blood, 'stid of the voice of the Almighty. 'No man, havin' put his hand to the plow and lookin' back, is fit fer the kingdom of God.' "

"I know, Grandpap," Ephraim murmured sadly, "but I can't decide agin her till I git more light."

On the young man's face a frown of sore perturbation still lingered, as he took his official place at the head of the rude table which, extending down the whole length of the meeting-house, held the steaming dishes of the sacred meal. Plates had been set for all the members of the church, who, as they filed in, sat down at the board, the men on one side and the women on the other.

The conscious color deepened in Ephraim's tanned cheek when his glance, wandering down the table, fell on a young girl seated near the opposite end. Among the faded or phlegmatic countenances around her, the rich bloom and vivacity of her face stood strongly out, reminding Ephraim of a crimson poppy he had once found gleaming amid the humbler growths of the garden. Like the rest of the women, she wore a plain frock of dark calico, and the white head-dress customary on sacramental occasions; but the muslin cap was fastened under her chin with a knot of warm-tinted ribbon, and below it glittered a huge breastpin, resplendent with gold plating and imitation jewels.

A sudden silence fell on the congregation as Ephraim rose and, laying aside his coat, girded a towel around him. Taking a basin of water, he knelt beside the man next him, who chanced to be Deacon Hunley, and washed and dried his feet. Then, rising, he bent his head and solemnly pressed on the old man's weazen lips the kiss of charity.

The shadows of the October afternoon deepened as the rite was passed from one to another around the table; and the first stars had come out above the dusky ridges when, the solemn meal ended, Ephraim made his way to Roxenie's side.

As he came up, his unsmiling eyes rested on a flashily-dressed young man who had been talking with the girl. "Good evenin', Abner," he said, coldly.

Abner Biddle, who, though born and bred a mountaineer, had for some years been employed on the public works at the county seat, had recently come back to the neighborhood of his birth, versed in so many ways of the world and displaying so many strange fashions, as might well dazzle the simple sons and daughters of Bays Mountain. It suddenly occurred to Ephraim that Roxenie's love of finery might have another source than the vanity natural to her years. "The world and the lusts thereof" all at once seemed to him to find concrete embodiment in Abner Biddle.

As Ephraim and Roxenie walked homeward along the

laurel-hedged path, the silence was for a time unbroken except by the wind in the pines, and the waters of Laurel Run, dashing over the rocks down the ravine.

At length the young man sighed deeply. "I 'm plumb disheartened about ye, Roxenie. It beats me why you should wear them gewgaws o' your'n to the Seckrement, of all places."

"I can't see as it 's wuss to wear 'em at Seckrement than anywhars else," the girl retorted. "I ain't a-goin' behind the door to hide what I do, and the whole church kin see ef they want to!"

"The whole church is a-seein' your acts, and a-grievin' fer 'em too! In fact," Ephraim's voice fell to an awed undertone, "ef you don't take heed to your ways, the Brethren 's a-talkin' about turnin' ye out!"

There was a startled hush, through which Roxenie could hear her own loud-beating heart. To dally with the forbidden allurements of the world from a position of supposed safety, had been diverting enough; but to be called to account, and turned out of the church as an unworthy member, was an appalling prospect, full of terror and shame.

"Who 's been talkin' about turnin' me out?" she demanded. "I 'low it 's old Jeremiah Hunley that's at the bottom of it! I seed you and him a-talkin' together, as thick as peas in a pod. And ye washed his feet, and give him the holy kiss! Lordy, ye must hev a strong stomach!"

"The foll'wers of the Lord ortn't to be above washin' nobody's feet, Roxenie. Whose feet did you wash—yer cousin Polly Ann Ledbetter's? That war one of the things the Brethern helt agin ye, that ye never washed nobody's feet at the Seckrement, onless it war some of yer own nigh kin."

"It 's Jeremiah Hunley's spite-work a-bringin' up sich things," the girl cried, passionately. "Atter him and pap had that fuss about the line-fence, he never war satisfied till he 'd got pap turned out o' the church; and he 'll never be satisfied now till he gits me turned out too."

"You nee'n't to lay it all on Jeremiah Hunley, nuther," Ephraim answered, stoutly. "It'll be yer own fault ef you 're turned out. You didn't hev to jine the Brethern, Roxenie; you could 'a' staid out ef you 'd 'a' wanted to; but bein' as you air a member, 'pears to me like you ort to do what you bound yerself up to!"

For a moment Roxenie was shocked into silence by the severity of her lover's words. Then her pride rose. "Yes, I could 'a' staid out of the church, Ephraim, and I 've wished a heap o' times that I hed! Thar ain't no use in bein' so quair, and different from everybody else! W'y, over in Kingsport, whar I went a-visitin' to Aunt Mirandy Pickens's, 'most every woman at the meetin'-house was a-wearin' gold pins; and they said when a gal promised to marry a feller, it war the reg'lar thing fer him to give her a ring. They 'lowed it war mighty quair that I was promised and didn't hev none, and I felt plumb ashamed." Roxenie laughed significantly. "Abner Biddle's got a pow'ful purty ring—"

She stopped abruptly as the rushing storm of Ephraim's wrath swept down on her. "Ef nothin' else'll do you, you kin hev Abner Biddle and his ring, fer all o' me. I 'll never buy a ring fer no woman while the world stands! I 've helt up fer you, Roxenie, and tuk your part agin them that was hard down on ye, but I 'll do it no more! I 've tried to snatch ye as a brand from the burnin', but from now on I'll leave ye to yer own ways. My skyirts is clear o' your blood!"

Roxenie's laugh rang out through the solemnity of the mountain night, clear and scornful, yet with something hollow and forced in its defiant tones. "Yes, your skyirts is clear, and so is Deacon Hunley's! Go ahead and turn me out ef you want to! Jeremiah Hunley'll never pull *me* around atter him with a leadin' string!"

A few days later, two or three Brethren chosen for that purpose called at the Pulliam cabin to talk with Roxenie, and endeavor to persuade her to submit to the church. They were received by Mrs. Pulliam, who, though she went through with all the essentials of mountain hospitality, setting "cheers" on the porch for the visitors, serving them with gourdfuls of water fresh from the spring, and inquiring minutely after their health and the health of their respective families, had about her a resolute frigidity that augured ill for the success of the visit. She was a rigid church member, and under other circumstances Roxenie's delinquencies and the prospect of her expulsion would have brought down a storm of lamentations and reproaches on the girl's head; but the supposition that Deacon Hunley was behind the movement to discipline Roxenie, awakening in the old woman dark memories of the grudge that had begun in her husband's lifetime, rendered her even more stubborn and defiant than her daughter.

"Jeremiah Hunley'll never run rough-shod over me and mine while my head 's hot," she had declared.

Roxenie listened to her visitors in silence, making to their exhortations the unvarying response that she hidn't done nothin' much wrong as she could see, and she wa'n't agoin' to make no acknowledgments to the church. The Brethren knew, as they walked down the rugged path from the house, that their mission had failed.

On the next preaching day, the meeting-house was crowded to overflowing; for the news that Roxenie Pulliam was to be "drawed before the brethen" had gone far and wide over the ridges, and even the most careless churchgoer had felt it incumbent on him to be present.

As the girl walked down the aisle on that eventful morning, there was a sudden stir of interest in the congregation, followed by a hush of utter amazement. Never before had such a vision appeared on Bays Mountain. Roxenie's calico dress and square cut, unfrilled Dunkard bonnet had been laid aside, and she shone dazzlingly forth in brilliant and heavily flounced sateen, while on her head rested the supreme sacrilege of a gaily trimmed hat bought at a fabulous price from a store in the valley. The much-offending breastpin flaunted itself on her bosom, and on one of her little brown hands glittered the blue stones of the ring Abner Biddle had given her. Something like a groan passed over the devouter portion of the congregation; and from that moment the result of the trial was foreseen.

During what followed, she sat haughtily erect. Only once did her resolution falter. When, at the close of the trial, Ephraim Utsman, as paster of the church, rose to pronounce the solemn sentence, her glance met his agonized face, turned in passionate pity upon her. Her head drooped for an instant, and a sudden tremor shook the blossoms on her gorgeous hat. Then she looked up as proudly as ever; and a defiant smile parted her lips as she passed through the crowd of brethren and sisters, to whose fellowship she belonged no more. It was not until she was well on her homeward road and the heavy underbrush had screened her from all eyes, that the angry pride which had sustained Roxenie fell away from her. The face above the scarlet ribbons grew strangely white; and the eyes she lifted to the accusing heavens were suddenly full of terror and remorse.

"O Lordy, what hev I done?" she moaned. "I 've give up Ephraim and lost my own soul, too, fer ought I know, all fer a passel of trash that ain't wuth no more 'n those dead leaves in the holler down yander!'

In a wild revulsion of feeling she tore off the brooch and the ring, and flung them far down the Laurel Run ravine.

"Roxenie Pulliam's reapin' the reward of her doin 's! It's a judgment of the Lord, ef ever I knowed of one!"

The speaker was a withered and rawboned old woman, who, on her way up the steep mountain road, had stopped to rest and chat at the corn pile, where the entire Utsman family were busy harvesting their fall crop. Ephraim and his father, with an old mule and a primitive "slide," were hauling the pumpkins and spindling corn down from the new ground on top of the ridge; while Mrs. Utsman and the younger children, a numerous company of all ages and sizes, were "shucking" the gathered ears and storing them in the crib.

At the visitor's words, uttered with an air of melancholy triumph befitting an annunciator of the judgments of the Lord, there was an astounded pause among the workers. Mr. Utsman, in the act of unloading a huge pumpkin, dropped it back on the sled; the children stood wide-eyed and open-mouthed, for once unrebuked by their mother for the suspension of their labors; and a gray shadow crept over Ephraim's face.

"Lordy, mussy," cried Mrs. Utsman, "I allus knowed that gal 'u'd come to no good eend! But tell us what's happened, Mis' Landers."

The news-bringer seated herself on the corn-pile, panting with excitement and the fatigue of her recent climb. "You-uns all know," she began, "about that thar ring, that Abner Biddle give Roxenie, and that she was a-flauntin' round so high, the day the brethren turned her out. Well, that ring war *stole!* Abner Biddle stole it from a man down about Rogersville that he'd been a-workin' fer. Thar ain't never been no sich ring in these parts afore. It was rale gold, and the sets in it war wuth away up yander, 'most fifty dollars!"

A gasp of astonishment went round the corn-pile. That there could be a ring worth fifty dollars had never occurred to the wildest imaginings of Bay Mountain.

"The feller that he stole it from," Mrs. Landers continued, "got to suspicionin' that mebbe Abner had tuk the ring, and so he come up here on a still hunt fer it. Do you mind that dressed-up man person, with eye-glasses, Mis' Utsman, that set at the back eend of the meetin'-house at Roxenie's trial? Well, that was him, and he seed his ring on the gal's hand that day. And this mornin', early, a officer rid up on hoss-back to Mis' Pulliam's, with a writ fer Roxenie. She's summoned fer trial over at Squair Riggs' on Beech Creek and the Lord only knows whar she 'll eend up at!"

"What's 'come of Abner Biddle?" demanded Ephraim, sternly. "Whar's the no-count pup that done the devilment, and then put it on Roxenie to tote his load!"

Mrs. Landers gazed on the young man with the icy severity justly due an interrupter of important news. "I don't know whar Abner Biddle is, and I hain't hed no pertickler call to find out. The officer stopped at his pap's, I heerd, but Abner hedn't been there since Sunday. But as fer as totin' Abner's load is concerned, Roxenie'll hev enough to do ef she totes her own load, accordin' to *my* count."

"The gal can't be sent to the pen, unless she tuk the ring a-known' it war stole."

Mr. Utsman, whose father had once been sheriff's deputy for a brief time, delivered this bit of inherited knowledge with befitting gravity. "But, o' course, she'll hev to restore the proputty."

The visitor bending forward lifted a mysteriously signifi-cant forefinger. "You-uns, mark my words," she said, her voice sinking to an impressive whisper, "Roxenie'll never

restore the proputty! She hain't got no notion of givin' up
that ring. Accordin' to her tale, she 's throwed it away and
can't find it no more!"

"Throwed it away!" exclaimed Mrs. Utsman, derisively.
"Don't tell me that a gal that loves finery like Roxenie Pulliam
does, would throw away a ring! She never would 'a' gone so
fur as to be turned out of the church fer it, ef she'd 'a' aimed
to throw it away."

"That's what I told 'em when I fust heerd it," corroborated
Mrs. Landers, "and everybody on Bays Mounting is a-sayin'
the same. Lordy, Lordy," the old woman shook her head
dismally, "when a immortal soul gits started down hill, thar
don't 'pear to be no stoppin'-place!"

Ephraim's face was tense with anguish, as he turned hur-
riedly away from the gossiping group. All the jealousy that
had stirred him on the night of his quarrel with Roxenie was
swallowed up in remorse for his delinquency as pastor, and
anxiety for the erring girl.

"Whatever she comes to, it's my fault, leastways part of it
is," he muttered. I ort n't never to 'a' forsook her when she
war so sore tempted. 'The hirelin' fleeth.' I han't been nothin'
but a hirelin' over the Lord's flock!"

An hour later, Roxenie was slowly descending the ridge on
her way to the 'Squire's for trial. Behind her came the
constable together with her uncle, Crit Ledbetter, who had
promised to accompany her to Beech Creek. She had chosen
to ride in advance in order, so far as possible, to escape the
old man's longwinded exhortations. "I 'low I'll be 'most glad
to go to the pen, jest to git shet of mam's and Uncle Crit's
jaw, fer a spell," she had declared, while a forlorn little smile
trembled on her pale lips.

Around her the words were bare in the desolation of late

autumn, and a blue haze, dim and infinitely mournful, filled the valleys and shrouded the distant peaks. As her eyes fell listlessly on the altered aspect of the autumnal woods, the girl's mind was occupied with more momentous changes. "Ain't it quair," she murmured, "how everything is turned round since we come along this road from the Seckrement! Jest five weeks ago a-Saturday, and it feels like fifty year!"

A horseman was approaching down one of the bridle-paths that led to the main road. Long before he reached her, Roxenie knew that it was Ephraim Utsman.

He drew back a moment at sight of the girl's stricken face. "You ort n't to git too much pestered about what 's happened," he said, gently. "Folks ain't apt to come to harm onless they mean harm theirselves. And I can't never believe you meant much wrong, Roxenie."

A gleam of surprise lighted the blank hopelessness of her countenance. "I don't know how come ye to say that, Ephraim. Thar ain't nary other soul on Bays Mounting that 's said as much. They all 'low it 's a made-up tale about losin' the ring, and say I'm a-keepin' it hid some'r's."

"What defence air ye aimin' to make afore the 'Squair?"

The girl's pale face grew paler.

"Folks is a-sayin'," she answered in a low, awed voice, "that it's a jedgment of the Lord that's come on me; and ef it is, it won't do no good to fight agin it. But I 'lowed, bein' as I'd throwed the man's ring away, I 'd ort to pay him fer it." Bending down, she laid a caressing hand on her mare's glossy neck. "Old Bet's wuth what the ring cost, and more too. Ef the man 'll be satisfied to take her in place of what he 's lost, we 'll be square; and ef he won't I 'm at the eend of my row," she added, despairingly.

"Roxenie," the young man's voice was full of passionate sorrow, "you ain't the only one that 's a-deservin' of the jedgment of the Most High! I 'm a-goin' with ye to the trial, and ef any harm befalls ye, I pray it may light on me, too. I war in fault. I turned agin ye and let ye stray from the Lord's fold, bekase I war mad and jealous, a-thinkin' ye loved Abner."

"Loved Abner!" Something of Roxenie's old spirit flashed into her eyes. "I ha'n't never been that bad off fer a feller yit! Ye must 'a' 'lowed I war purty fur gone, to take up with the likes of Abner Biddle!"

A sudden light came into Ephraim's troubled face. "Tell me why you throwed the ring away, Roxenie!" he demanded, eagerly. "Could it 'a' been bekase ye hated it—bekase ye war sorry fer what ye 'd done?"

Roxenie's composure, which she had kept so resolutely through all that had befallen, was giving way at last. Dropping the reins on her mare's neck, she buried her face in her hands. "Sorry! O Ephraim," she sobbed, "you can't know—nobody can't know—how sorry I was!"

It was nearly ten o'clock on the following morning when Mrs. Pulliam, coming to the door, peered out with eyes that were red from a night of weeping. Many times, during the past twenty-four hours, she had thus stepped forth, scanning the narrow road, or listening intently for every footstep or distant barking of dogs that might foretoken news of Roxenie. Now, as she stood on the porch, listening, she fancied she heard the sound of hoofs coming up from the hollow; and a few moments later, Crit Ledbetter's mule appeared over the slope.

When she saw that Roxenie was not with her uncle, the old woman threw her apron over her head, and broke into loud lamentation. "I knowed it 'u'd turn out that way!" she wailed. "I knowed when the pore gal started off, that she 'd never set foot on Bays Mounting agin!"

Crit Ledbetter gave a bluff, reassuring laugh, "You nee'n't to pester nary bit about Roxenie. She 's a-comin' on behind, and old Bet 's a-comin' too. The feller that Abner stole from war a pow'ful clever man. When Roxenie d' told him all about the ring, and offered him the old mare to make up fer it, he would n't hev the nag at all. He said he 'd like mightly well to git a holt of the rascal that stole his proputty, but he didn't hev no notion of sendin' a innicent gal to the pen, nor of takin' a widder woman's hoss, nuther. And he hed the trial called right spang off, and paid the costs hisself!"

"Air ye tellin' me the truth, Crit?" the old woman cried, incredulously. "Ef nothin's happened to Roxenie, why hain't she come back along o' you?"

A sly smile wrinkled Crit Ledbetter's brown visage. "The gal 's all right," he answered, "but they was delayed by hevin' to wait till the license come from town. You see, atter the trial was called off, her and Ephraim 'lowed they 'd git married while they was over thar, bein' as thar wa'n't no use in makin' all that long trip to the 'Squair's fer nothin'!"

POETRY

   ~ ~ ~

ROSEMARY AND PANSIES

DEDICATION
TO THE MEMORY OF MY
BROTHER MARVIN

AT THE GRAVE OF ONE FORGOTTEN

In a churchyard old and still,
Where the breeze-touched branches thrill
  To and fro,
Giant oak trees blend their shade
O'er a sunken grave-mound, made
  Long ago.

No stone, crumbling at its head,
Bears the mossed name of the dead
  Graven deep;
But a myriad blossoms' grace
Clothes with trembling light the place
  Of his sleep.

Was a young man in his strength
Laid beneath this low mound's length,
  Heeding naught?
Did a maiden's parents wail
As they saw her, pulseless, pale,
  Hither brought?

Was it else one full of days,
Who had traveled darksome ways,
  And was tired,
Who looked forth unto the end,

First published by the Gorham Press, Boston, Massachusetts, 1909.

And saw Death come as a friend
    Long desired?

Who it was that rests below
Not earth's wisest now may know,
    Or can tell;
But these blossoms witness bear
They who laid the sleeper there
    Loved him well.

In the dust that closed him o'er
Planted they the garden store
    Deemed most sweet,
Till the fragrant gleam, outspread,
Swept in beauty from his head
    To his feet.

Still, in early springtime's glow,
Guelder-roses cast their snow
    O'er his rest;
Still sweet-williams breathe perfume
Where the peonies' crimson bloom
    Drapes his breast.

Passing stranger, pity not
Him who lies here, all forgot,
    'Neath this earth;
Some one loved him—more can fall
To no mortal. Love is all
    Life is worth.

THE SHEPHERDS' VISION *

Upon the dim Judean hills,
   The shepherds watched their flock by night,
When on their unexpectant gaze
   Outshone that vision of delight,
The fairest that did ever rise
To awe and gladden earthy eyes.

From no far realm those shepherds came,
   Treading the pilgrim's weary road;
Not theirs the vigil and the fast
   Within the hermit's mean abode;
'Twas at their usual task they stood,
When dawned that light of matchless good.

Not only to the sage and seer
   Life's revelation comes in grace;
Most often on the toiler true,
   Who, working steadfast in his place,
Looks for the coming of God's will,
The glorious vision shineth still.

HEREDITY

Our dead forefathers, mighty though they be,
For all their power still leave our spirits free;
Though on our paths their shadows far are thrown,
The life that each man liveth is his own.

Time stands like some schoolmaster old and stern,
And calls each human being in his turn

* First published in the *Independent* 65 (24 Dec. 1908): 1521.

To write his task upon life's blackboard space;
Death's fingers then the finished work erase,
And the next pupil's letters take its place.

That he who wrote before thee labored well
Concerns thee not: thy work for thee must tell;
    'Tis naught to thee if others' tasks were ill:
Thou hast thy chance and canst improve it still.
From all thy fathers' glory and their guilt
The board for thee is clean: write what thou wilt!

THE WOOD FIRE

O giant oak, majestic, dark, and old,
    A hundred summers in the woodland vast,
    From the rich suns that lit thy glories past,
In thy huge trunk thou storedst warmth untold;
Now, when the drifted snows the hills enfold,
    And the wild woods are shaken in the blast,
    O'er this bright hearth thou sendest out at last
The long-pent sunshine that thine heart did hold.

Like thee, O Noble oak-tree, I would store
    From days of joy all beauty and delight,
    All radiant warmth that makes life's summer bright,
So that I may, when sunniest hours are o'er,
Still from my heart their treasured gleam outpour,
    To cheer some spirit in its winter night.

A NEW YEAR'S HOPE

I dare not hope that in this dawning year
I shall accomplish all my dreams hold dear;
That I, when this year closes, shall have wrought
All the high tasks that my ambitions sought,
And that I shall be then the spirit free,
Strong, and unselfish, that I long to be.

But truly do I hope, resolve, and pray
That, as the new year passes, day by day
My footsteps, howsoever short and slow,
Shall still press forward in the path they go,
And that my eyes, uplifted evermore,
Shall look forth dauntless to the things before;
And when this new year with the old has gone,
I still may courage have to struggle on.

TO A SILVER DOLLAR

Pale coin, what various hands have you passed through
    Ere you to-day within my hand were laid?
    Perchance a laborer's well-earned hire you made;
Some miser may have gloated long on you;
Perhaps some pitying hand to Want outthrew;
    And, lost and won through devious tricks of trade,
    You may have been, alas! the full price paid
For some pour soul that loved you past your due.

No doubt 'tis well, O imaged Liberty,
    You see not where your placid face is thrust,
Nor know how far man is from being free,
    Bound as he is by money's fateful lust,

While to his anxious soul like mockery
   Seem those fair, graven words: "In God we trust."

PREPARATION

"I have no time for those things now," we say;
"But in the future just a little way,
No longer by this ceaseless toil oppressed,
I shall have leisure then for thought and rest.
When I the debts upon my land have paid,
Or on foundations firm my business laid,
I shall take time for discourse long and sweet
With those beloved who round my hearthstone meet;
I shall take time on mornings still and cool
To seek the freshness dim of wood and pool,
Where, calmed and hallowed by great Nature's peace,
My life from its hot cares shall find release;
I shall take time to think on destiny,
Of what I was and am and yet shall be,
Till in the hush my soul may nearer prove
To that great Soul in whom we live and move.
All this I shall do sometime but not now—
The press of business cares will not allow."
And thus our life glides on year after year;
The promised leisure never comes more near.
Perhaps the aim on which we placed our mind
Is high, and its attainment slow to find;
Or if we reach the mark that we have set,
We still would seek another, farther yet.
Thus all our youth, our strength, our time go past
Till death upon the threshold stands at last,
And back unto our Maker we must give
The life we spent preparing well to live.

GHOSTS

Upon the eve of Bosworth, it is said,
  Until Richard waited through the drear night's gloom
  Until wan morn the death-field should illume,
Those he had murdered came with soundless tread
To daunt his soul with prophecies of dread,
  And bid him know that, gliding from the tomb,
  They would fight 'gainst him in his hour of doom
Until with theirs should lie his discrowned head.

To every man, in life's decisive hour,
  Ghosts of the past do through the conflict glide,
And for him or against him wield their power;
  Lost hopes and wasted days and aims that died
Rise spectral where the fateful war-clouds lower,
  And their pale hands the battle shall decide.

THE RAINBOW

Love is a rainbow that appears
When heaven's sunshine lights earth's tears.

All varied colors of the light
Within its beauteous arch unite:

There Passion's glowing crimson hue
Burns near Truth's rich and deathless blue;

And Jealousy's green lights unfold
'Mid Pleasure's tints of flame and gold.

O dark life's stormy sky would seem,
If love's clear rainbow did not gleam!

HEROES

Men, for the sake of those they loved,
　　Have met death unafraid,
Deeming by safety of their friends
　　Their life's loss well repaid.

Men have attained, by dauntless toil,
　　To purpose pure and high,
The darkness of their rugged ways
　　Lit by a loved one's eye.

Heroes were they, yet God to them
　　Gave not the task most hard,
For sweet it is to live or die
　　When love is our reward.

The bravest soul that ever lived
　　Is he, unloved, unknown,
Who has chosen to walk life's highest path,
　　Though he must walk alone;

Who has toiled with sure and steadfast hands
　　Through all his lonely days,
Unhelped by Love's sweet services,
　　Uncheered by Love's sweet praise;

Who, by no earthly honors crowned,
　　Kinglike has lived and died,
Giving his best to life, through life
　　To him her best denied.

THE RECOMPENSE

O ancient ocean, with what courage stern
   Thy tides, since time began, have sought to gain
   The luring moon, toward which they rise in vain,
Yet daily to their futile aim return.
Like thee do glorious human spirits yearn
   And strive and fail and strive and fail again
   Some starlike aspiration to attain,
Some light that ever shall above them burn.

Yet truly shall their recompense abide
   To all who strive, although unreached their goal:
The ceaseless surgings of the ocean tide
   Do cleanse the mighty waters which they roll,
And the high dreams in which it vainly sighed
   Make pure the deeps of the aspiring soul.

THE TEST

"He fears not death, and therefore he is brave"—
   How common yet how childish is the thought,
   As if death were the hardest battle fought,
And earth held naught more dreadful than the grave!

In life, not death, doth lie the brave soul's test,
   For life demandeth purpose long and sure,
   The strength to strive, the patience to endure;
Death calls for one brief struggle, then gives rest.

Through our fleet years then let us do our part
   With willing arm, clear brain, and steady nerve;
   In death's dark hour no spirit true will swerve,
If he have lived his life with dauntless heart.

TO A DEAD BABY

Pale little feet, grown quiet ere they could run
    One step in life's strange journey; sweet lips chilled
    To silence ere they prattled; small hands stilled
Before one stroke of life's long toil was done;
Uncreased white brows that laurels might have won,
    Yet leave their spacious promise unfulfilled—
    O baby dead, I cannot think God willed
Your life should end when it had scarce begun!

If no man died till his long life should leave
    All hopes and aims fulfilled, until his feet
Had trod all paths where men rejoice or grieve,
    I might have doubt of future life more sweet;
But as I look on you, I must believe
    There is a heaven that makes this earth complete.

THANKSGIVING

Our Father, whose unchanging love
    Gives soil and sun and rain,
We thank Thee that the seeds we sowed
    Were planted not in vain,
But that Thy hand the year hath crowned
    With wealth of fruits and grain.

But more we thank Thee for the hope
    Which hath our solace been,
That when the harvests of our lives
    Have all been gathered in,
Our weary hearts and toil-worn hands
    Thy welcoming smile shall win.

We thank Thee for the cheerful board
   At which fond faces meet,
And for the human loves that make
   Our transient years so sweet;
We thank Thee most for hopes of heaven
   Where love shall be complete.

Though on some dear, remembered face
   No more the hearth lights shine,
We thank Thee that the friends we loved
   Are kept by love divine,
And though they pass beyond our gaze,
   They do not pass from Thine.

If at the harvest feast no more
   Our words and smiles shall blend,
We thank Thee that, though sundered far,
   Our steps still homward tend,
And that our Father's open door
   Awaits us at the end.

UNDER ROOFS

Between us and the starred vasts overhead
Broad-builded roofs we spread,
Thus shutting from our view the wonders high
Of the clear midnight sky;
Yet all our roofs make not more faint or far
One ray of one dim star.

Our souls build o'er them roofs of dread and doubt,
   And think they shut God out;
Yet all the while, remembering though forgot,
That vast Love, changing not,
Abides, and, spite of all our faithless fear,
Shines nevermore less near.

FOREVER

We sigh for human love, from which
    A whim or chance shall sever,
And leave unsought the love of God,
    Though God's love lasts forever.

We seek earth's peace in things that pass
    Like foam upon the river,
While, steadfast as the stars on high.
    God's peace abides forever.

Man's help, for which we yearn, gives way,
    As trees in storm-winds quiver,
But, mightier than all human need,
    God's help remains forever.

Turn unto Thee our wavering hearts,
    O Thou who failest never;
Give us Thy love and Thy great peace,
    And be our Help forever!

IF CHRIST SHOULD COME

If Christ should come to my store to-day,
What would he think, what would he say?
If his eyes on my opened ledgers were laid,
Would they meet a record of unfair trade,
And see that, lured by the love of pelf,
For a trivial price I had sold myself?
Or would he the stainless record behold
Of perfect integrity, richer than gold?

If Christ should come to my school-room to-day,
What would he think, what would he say?
Would he find me giving the self-same care
To stupid and poor as to rich and fair,
And striving, unmindful of praise or blame,
Through tedious tasks to a lofty aim,
Guiding small feet as they forward plod
In paths of duty that lead to God?

If Christ should come to my workshop to-day,
What would he think, what would he say?
Would his eye, as it glanced my work along,
See that all its parts were stanch and strong,
Closely fitted, firm-welded, and good,
Of flawless steel and of unwarped wood,
As sound as I trust my soul shall be
When tried by the test of eternity?

If Christ should come to my kitchen to-day,
What would he think, what would he say?
Would he find me with blithesome and grateful heart
And hands well-skilled in the housewife's art,
Bearing sordid cares with a spirit sweet,
And making the lowliest tasks complete?

Cometh he not, who of old did say,
"Lo, I am with you, my friends, always"?
O thought that our weary hearts must thrill,
In our toilsome ways he is present still!
At counter and forge, in office and filed,
He stands, to no mortal eye revealed.

Ah, if we only could realize
That ever those gentle yet searching eyes
Gaze on our work with approval or blame,

Our slipshod lives would not be the same!
For, thrilled by the gaze of the unseen Guest,
In our daily toil we would do our best.

GIFTS

Myrrh and frankincense and gold—
Thus the ancient story told—
When the seers found Him they sought,
To the wondrous babe they brought.
Let us—ours the selfsame quest—
Bear unto the Christ our best.

If to him, as to our King,
We the gift of gold would bring,
Be it royal offering!
Gold unstained by stealth or greed,
Gold outflung to all earth's need,
That hath softened human woe—
Helped the helpless, raised the low.

Frankincense for him is meet,
Yet no Orient odors sweet
Are to him as fragrant gift
As white thoughts to God uplift,
And a life that soars sublime,
Sweet above ill scents of time.

Last, from out the Magians' store,
Myrrh, as for one dead, they bore;
While, perchance, their lifted eyes
Viewed afar the Sacrifice.
Let us to the sepulcher

Bring a richer gift than myrrh:
Love that will not yield to dread
When all human hopes have fled;
Faith that falters not nor quails
When the waning earth-light fails,
Saying, "Shall I be afraid
Of the dark where Thou wast laid?"

BENEFACTION

If thou the lives of men wouldst bless,
live thine own life in faithfulness;
Thine own hard task, if made complete,
Shall render others' toil more sweet;

Thy grief, if bravely thou endure,
Shall give men's sorrow solace sure;
Thy peril, if met undismayed,
Shall make the fearful less afraid.

Each step in right paths firmly trod
Shall break some thorn or crush some clod,
Making the way more smooth and free
For him who treads it after thee.

HISTORIC GROUND

No song lends these calm vales a deathless name;
   No hero, to a nation's honors grown,
   Claims as his birthplace these rude hills unknown;
No pomp of hostile armies ever came,

Marring these fields with storied blood and flame;
   And yet the darkest tragedies of time,
   Of love and death the mysteries sublime
Have thrilled this tranquil spot, unmarked of fame.

Here the long conflict between good and ill
   Has been fought out to shame or victory,
   Darkly and madly as in scenes renowned.
Ah, though unnamed in human records, still
Within the annals of eternity
   This place obscure is true historic ground!

A MOUNTAIN GRAVEYARD

What a sleeping-place is here!
O vast mountain, grim and drear,
Though, throughout their life's hard round,
To thy sons, in long toil bound,
Thou from stony hill and field
Didst a scanty sustenance yield,
Surely thou art kinder now!
Here, beneath the gray cliff's brow,
Sleep they in the hemlocks' gloom,
And no king has prouder tomb.

Far above the clustered mounds,
Through the trees the faint wind sounds,
Waking in each dusky leaf
Sobs of immemorial grief;
And while silent years pass by,
Dark boughs lifted toward the sky
Like wild arms appealing toss,
As if they were mad with loss,

And with human hearts did share
Grief's long protest and despair.

No tall marbles, gleaming white,
Here reflect the softened light;
Yet beside the hillocks green
Rude, uncarven stones are seen,
Brought there from the mountain side
By the mourners' love and pride.
There, too, scattered o'er the grass
Of the graves, are bits of glass
That with white shells mingled lie.
Smile not, ye who pass them by,
For the love that placed them there
Deemed that they were things most fair.

Now, when from their souls at last
Life's long paltriness has passed,
The unending strife for bread
That has stunted heart and head,
These tired toilers may forget
All earth's trivial care and fret.
Haply death may give them more
Than they ever dreamed before,
And may recompense them quite
For all lack of life's delight;
Death may to their gaze unbar
Summits vaster, loftier far
Than the blue peaks that surround
This still-shadowed burial ground.

AFTER THE LAST LESSON

How wonderful he seems to me,
 Now that the lessons are all read,
And, smiling through the stillness dim,
 The child I taught lies dead!

I was his teacher yesterday—
 Now, could his silent lips unclose,
What lessons might he teach to me
 Of the vast truth he knows!

Last week he bent his anxious brows
 O'er maps with puzzling Poles and Zone;
Now he, perchance, knows more than all
 The scientists have known.

"Death humbleth all"—ah, say not so!
 The man we scorn, the child we teach
Death in a moment places far
 Past all earth's lore can reach.

Death bringeth men unto their own!
 He tears aside Life's thin disguise,
And man's true greatness, all unknown,
 Stands clear before our eyes.

THE ROAD TO CHURCH

Rutted by wheels and scarred by hoofs
 And by rude footsteps trod,
The old road winds through glimmering woods
 Unto the house of God.

How many feet, assembling here
  From each diverse abode,
Led by how many different aims,
  Have walked this shadowy road!

How many sounds of woe and mirth
  Have thrilled these green woods dim—
The funeral's slow and solemn tramp,
  The wedding's joyous hymn.

Full oft, amid the gloom and glow
  Through which the highway bends,
I watch the meeting streams of life,
  Whose mingled current tends

Toward where, beyond the rock-strewn hill,
  Against the dusky pines
That rise above the churchyard graves,
  The white spire soars and shines.

Here pass bowed men, with blanching locks,
  World-weary, faint, and old,
Mourning the ways of reckless youths
  Far-wandering from the fold.

There totter women, frail and meek,
  Of dim but gentle eyes,
Whom heaven's love has made most kind,
  Earth's hardships made most wise.

Apart, two lovers walk together,
  With words and glances fond,
So happy now they scarce can feel
  The need of bliss beyond.

Gaunt-limbed, his shoulders stooped with toil,
  His forehead seamed with care,
Adown the road the farm hand stalks
  With awed and awkward air.

The sermon glimmers in his mind,
  Its truth half understood,
And yet from prayer and hymn he gains
  A shadowy dream of good

That sanctifies the offering
  His bare life daily makes—
His tender love for wife and child,
  And toil borne for their sakes.

Thus through the bleakness and the bloom,
  O'er snows and freshening grass,
Devout, profane, grief-worn or gay,
  The thronged church-goers pass,

Till, one by one, they each and all,
  Their earthly journeyings o'er,
Move silent down that well-known road
  Which they shall walk no more.

THE PATCHWORK QUILT

In an ancient window seat,
Where the breeze of morning beat
'Gainst her face, demure and sweet,
Sat a girl of long ago,
With her sunny head bent low
Where her fingers flitted white
Through a maze of patchwork bright.

Wondrous hues the rare quilt bears!
All the clothes the household wears
By their fragments may be traced
In that bright mosaic placed;
Pieces given by friend and neighbor,
Blended by her curious labor
With the grandame's gown of gray,
And the silken bonnet gay
That the baby's head hath crowned,
In the quaint design are found.

Did she aught suspect or dream,
As she sewed each dainty seam,
That a haunted thing she wrought?
That each linsey scrap was fraught
With some tender memory
Which, in distant years to be,
Would lost hopes and loves recall,
When her eyes should on it fall?

Years have passed, and with their grace
Gentler made her gentle face;
Brilliant still the fabrics shine
Of the quilt's antique design,
As she folds it, soft and warm,
Round a fair child's sleeping form.
Lustrous is her lifted gaze
As with half-voiced words she prays
That the bright head on that quilt
May not bow in shame or guilt,
And the little feet below
Darksome paths may never know.

Yet again the morning shines
On the patch-work's squares and lines;

Dull and dim its colors show,
But more dim the eyes that glow,
Wandering with a dreamy glance
O'er the ancient quilt's expanse;
Worn its textures are and frayed,
But the hands upon them laid,
Creased with toils of many a year,
Still more worn and old appear.

But what hands, long-loved and dead,
Do those faded fingers, spread
O'er those faded fabrics, meet
In reunion fond and sweet!
What past scenes of tenderness
And of joy that none may guess,
Called back by the patchwork old,
Do those darkening eyes behold!
Lo, the deathless past comes near!
From the silence whisper clear
Long-hushed tones, and, changing not,
Forms and faces unforgot
In their old-time grace and bloom
Shine out from the deepening gloom.

MY BROTHER
(1882–1903)

Dead! and he has died so young.
Silent lips, with song unsung,
Still hands, with the field untilled,
Lofty purpose unfulfilled.

Was that life so incomplete?
Strong heart, that no more shall beat,

Ardent brain and glorious eye,
That seemed meant for tasks so high,
But now moulder back to earth,
Were you all then nothing worth?

Could the death-dew and the dark
Quench that soul's unflickering spark?
Are its aims, so high and just,
All entombed here in the dust?

O, we trust God shall unfold
More than earthly eyes behold,
And that they whose years were fleet
Find life's promises complete,
Where, in lands no gaze hath met,
Those we grieve for love us yet!

IN FULLER MEASURE

"Dying so young, how much he missed!" they said,
  While his unbreathing sleep they wept around;
  "If he had lived, Fame surely would have crowned
With wreath of fadeless green his kingly head;
The clear glance of his burning eyes had read
  Wisdom's dim secrets, hoary and profound;
  While his life's path would have been holy ground,
Made thus by all men's love upon it shed."

Doubtless could he have spoken for whom that rain
  Of teardrops fell, "How strange your sad words are!"
  He would have said; "In fuller measure far
All that life gave to me I still retain;
  Love have I now which no dark longings mar,
Fame void of strife, and wisdom free from pain."

OCTOBER

O sweetest month, that pourest from full hands
The golden bounty of rich harvest lands!
O saddest month, that bearest with thy breath
The crimson leaves to drifts of glowing death!

In fields and lives, the fall of withered leaves
Darkens the glorious season of ripe sheaves,
For Life's fruition comes with loss and pain,
And Death alone can bring the richest gain.

BENIGNANT DEATH *

Thanking God for life and light,
   Strength and joyous breath,
Should we not, with reverent lips,
   Thank Him, too, for death?

When would man's injustice cease,
   Did not stern Death bring
Those who cheated and oppressed
   To their reckoning?

Would not life's long sordidness
   On our spirits pall,
If our years should last forever,
   And the earth were all?

On us, withered with life's heat,
   Falls death's cooling dew,

* First published in *Putnam's Monthly* 5 (Dec. 1908): 334.

And our parched souls' dusty leaves
  Their lost green renew.

Ah, though deep the grave-dust hide
  Love and courage high,
Life a paltrier thing would be
  If we could not die!

THE UNRETURNING

If our dead could come back to us,
  Who so desire it,
And be as they were before,
  Would we require it?

Would we bid them share again
  Our weakness, foregoing
All their higher blessedness
  Of being and knowing?

For them the triumph is won,
  The fight completed;
Do we wish that the doubtful strife
  Should be repeated?

Would we call them from the calm
  Of all assurance
To the perils that might prove
  Past their endurance?

God is kind, since He will not heed
  Our bitter yearning,
And the gates of heaven are shut
  'Gainst all returning.

WHEN A HUNDRED YEARS HAVE PASSED

When a hundred years have passed,
What shall then be left at last
Of us and the deeds we wrought?
Shall there be remaining aught
Save green graves in churchyards old,
Names o'ergrown with moss and mold,
From the worn stones half effaced,
And from human hearts erased?

When a hundred years have fled,
Will it matter how we sped
In the conflicts of to-day,
Which side took we in the fray,
If we dared or if we quailed,
If we nobly won or failed?
It will matter! If, too weak
For the right to strike or speak,
We in virtue's cause are dumb,
Some soul in far years to come
Shall have darker strife with vice,
Weakened by our cowardice.
Every struggle that we make,
Every valiant stand we take
In a righteous cause forlorn,
Shall give strength to hearts unborn.

When a hundred years have gone,
Darkness and oblivion
Shall our ended lives obscure,
But their influence shall endure.
Other eyes shall be upraised

To the hills on which we gazed,
And the paths o'er which we plod
Shall be other feet be trod,
While our names shall be forgot;
Yet, although they know it not,
Those who live then, none the less,
We shall sadden or shall bless.
They shall bear our boon or curse,
They shall better be or worse,
As we who shall then lie still,
Have lived nobly or lived ill.

FALLEN LEAVES

Beneath the frost-stripped forest boughs, the
    drifted leaves are spread,
Vanished all summer's green delight, all
    autumn's glory fled.

Yet, gathering strength from that dead host,
    the tree in some far spring
Shall toward the skies a denser growth, a
    darker foliage fling.

Ah, if some power from us, long dead, should
    strengthen life to be,
We need not grieve to lie forgot, like sere
    leaves 'neath the tree!

DECEMBER SNOW

The falling snow a stainless veil doth cast
   Upon the relics of the dying year—
   Dead leaves and withered flowers and stubble sere—
As if it would erase the faded past;
So on our lives does death descend at last,
   Hiding youth's hopes and manhood's purpose clear,
   And memories faint, to dreaming age most dear,
Beneath its silence, blank and white and vast.

The sun shines out, and lo! the meadows lone
   Flash into sudden splendor, strangely bright,
More fair than summer landscape ever shone;
   Thus, gleaming through the storm clouds faith's clear light
   Transforms death's endless waste of silence white
To beauty passing all that life has known.

TRUST

I came, I go, at His behest,
So, fearing not and not distressed,
I pass unto that life unguessed.

Little the babe, at its first cry,
Knows of the scenes that near it lie;
Less still of that dim life know I.

But Love receives the babe to earth,
Soft hands give welcome at its birth;
And so I think, when I go forth,

There too shall wait, to cheer and bless,
Love, warm as mother's first caress,
Strong as a father's tenderness.

TOWARD SUNRISE

When, in old days, our fathers came
   To bury low their dead,
Unto the far-off eastern sky
   They turned the narrow bed.

They laid the sleeper on his couch
   With firm and simple faith
That cloudless morn would surely come
   To end the night of death;

And thus they sought to place him where,
   When life's clear sun should rise,
Its earliest rays might wakening fall
   Across his close-sealed eyes.

Like a faint fragrance lingering on
   Throughout unnumbered years,
Still in our country burial-grounds
   The custom sweet appears;

Still, when the light of life from eyes
   Beloved is withdrawn,
The sleepers' dreamless beds are made
   Facing the looked-for dawn.

There, as the seasons pass, they seem
   Serenely to await
The certain radiance of that Morn
   That cometh soon or late.

GOOD NIGHT

Dear earth, I am going away to-night
From your long-loved hills and your meadows bright;
I know I should miss you when I am dead
If a better world came not in your stead.

For the sweet, long days in your woodlands spent,
And your starry dusks, I shall not lament;
For greater than all the wonders you show,
O earth, is the secret I soon shall know.

Good night! And now as I fall asleep
I give you the garment I wore to keep;
You will hold it safely till morning dawn
And I rise from my slumber to put it on.

THE FADED BLOSSOMS

One gazed back sadly on his years withdrawn,
    The glad, fair, hopeful years that never yet
    Had borne the marks of error or regret;
Pure as the page that ne'er was written on,
Or cherry blossoms in spring's tender dawn;
    "Alas," he grieved, "life's page no more is white,
    Life's blossom now is faded as with blight.
The stainless freshness of my youth is gone.

And yet the tree's true purpose is not bloom:
The white flower withers that the fruit may come:
The page lacks meaning till on it is traced
The deep-lined word; yea tho by blots defaced
If ours be writ with courage and with truth,
We need not mourn the unsoiled blank of youth.

Independent 11 (20 July 1911): 128.

AUTUMN WINDS

O autumn winds, with voices far away,
   I hear you singing on the leafless hills,
And all my heart with jubilation thrills!
You bring to me no message of dismay,
No tender sorrow for the year's decay;
   Rather you sing of giant trees that cast
   Their leaves aside to grapple with the blast,
Strong and exultant for the stormy fray!

Hearing your music, glad and wild and pure,
   Sounding through night's cool, starlit spaces wide,
I grow aweary of earth's paltry lure!
   Oh, like the trees, I too would cast aside
   The fading leaves of pleasure and of pride,
And stand forth free to struggle and endure!

Harper's Magazine 135 (Sept. 1917): 536.

SONGS of the MONTHS

By EFFIE WALLER

PUBLISHED BY BROADWAY
PUBLISHING COMPANY
835 BROADWAY, NEW YORK

TO THE READER.

When stretching meadow-land
Was fresh and verdure-spanned,
By Summer's breezes fanned;
Beneath its spreading elms,
   Far from the noisy town,
In thoughtful meditation there
   I've often laid me down.

And o'er green-wooded hills,
Atune with wild-bird trills,
Mingling with prattling rills,
I've wandered oftentimes
   Beside the rillet's edge,
Or sat me down to think and dream
   On moss and fern-clad ledge.

Sometimes beside the river
Where alders quake and quiver,
Where pipe-reeds shake and shiver,
Beneath the sycamores
   From care and labor free
Upon the lush green grass I've sat
   In thoughtful reverie.

There musing oft at night
When clear and soft the light
Fell from the stars so bright,
I've wandered solitary,
   When Nature seemed at ease,
When soft and low the cooing gales
   Whispered among the trees.

I've sat 'neath orchard trees
When sighed September's breeze,
And heard the hum of bees,
Busy at apple paring.
   And at the apple-kiln,
Or feeding and relieving
   The pond'rous cider-mill.

When the birds had southward flown,
When leaves fell gently down,
Leaves yellow, red and brown
When to a somber color
   Had changed the once green hedge.
When spires of blood-red sumacs glowed
   Around the pasture's edge.

And when north winds did blow
And heap the driving snow,
While fires did brightly glow;
Then oftentimes surrounded
   By narrow kitchen walls.
And oftentimes 'mid cloister life
   And oft in classic halls.

To the Reader.

Within my room sometimes
I've sat me down to rhymes
Æsthetic and sublime
While on my desk were school books
  So careless piled and laid,
The morrow's problems all unsolved,
  The history unread.

Amid such scenes and through
Rude circumstances, too,
These lines I give to you,
Were written, and I hope they'll get
  Your criticism just;
And after reading of them
  You'll feel repaid, I trust.

THE AUTHOR.

INDEX.

INTRODUCTION.

MODEST worth, nobility of character, virtue, and truth, require no ornament, but themselves command admiration, whether the one who possesses them be of the most humble origin or of princely birth.

The writer of these lines sees such a person in the young author of this volume, whose origin was of the most humble, being Ethiopian, and whose parents were slaves.

The present writer is of Anglo-Saxon race, strongly imbued with Southern prejudices, and whose near relatives, the Elliotts of Eastern Kentucky, fought to keep the negro in subjection.

But time and the development of the colored race will surely appeal to the reason of the anti-Abolitionists and cause them to reflect that perhaps after all they may have been in error. Be that as it may, our intention is to discuss briefly the author and the merits of her book. Miss Waller is the daughter of poor, but highly respected colored people, has one brother and one sister who possess unusual mentality, and are numbered among the best teachers in the South. Miss Effie, the author of this book, as well as the others, had quite a struggle to acquire an educa-

tion. Being the youngest, she was kept away
from school during a great portion of each term,
since the only colored school in this whole section was situated at Pikeville, several miles distant from her former home. But she pursued
her studies with her mother's help, and attended
school as regularly as she could, and finally was
able to obtain a teacher's certificate.

She then began to teach, taking the money
she saved, and paying her expenses at the Colored State Normal School, at Frankfort, until
she has obtained an excellent education, and she
expects to still press forward until she has fully
completed it.

Miss Waller's poems, as all who read them
will observe, are possessed of much pathos and
beauty, having an originality all their own. Who
knows, that like Paul Lawrence Dunbar she may
not one day surprise and delight her own race,
and cause white critics to wonder at her genius.

She displays much rhythmic talent in the poem
"In Memory of W. Hughs," a dead classmate,
from which the following is taken:

"It was in the month of June, and the woods
    were all atune.
  All atune with bird music sweet and rare;
And the flowers were all in bloom, shedding
    forth their sweet, rich perfume
  On the breezy atmosphere everywhere."

Then she touchingly refers to their meeting
at that time, and of their future association, and
the last stanza runs like this:

"Little thought I, friend of mine,
You'd be called so soon to shine
In that galaxy of diadems up there;
But it was our Father's will
And He speaks to-day: 'Be still!'
To my sad and sorrow-stricken heart down
here."

The scholarly Rev. Peter Clay, a writer of great ability, and who knows our gifted little poet, a few years ago gave vent to his admiration in rhyme as follows:

TO EFFIE WALLER.

"Far up among the mountains,
Where rivers leave their fountains,
And happy birds send forth their merry thrills;
There dwells a little poet,
Though few there be who know it,
Whose voice is an echo from the hills.

"You may not like her station,
For she is not Caucasian,
Yet God with music touched the singer's heart;
And thoughts in liquid measure
Doth flow out like a treasure,
To charm us with the poet's mystic art."

In Miss Waller's verse there is that simply beautiful, lyrical quality, by which Keats and Burns charm and win all hearts.

A competent New York critic, Mr. S. G. Clow, says of Miss Waller's book:

"Here indeed are poems written close to nature's heart!

"Rarely have we seen such faithful, loving pictures, as within the covers of this charming book, of nature in all her moods and of simple homelike things, which steal us away from the city's din back to the country lanes and the old kitchen porch which we knew so long ago. . . . . By this beautiful anthology Miss Waller has done credit and honor to her race. Like her gifted compatriot, Paul Lawrence Dunbar, she will do much to dissolve the foolish prejudice of color, and to prove that poetic genius is the heritage of their race as well as ours.

"A unique, a wonderful book! If you desire a breath of odorous country air fresh from the dear old Southland you must read it!"

MARY ELLIOTT FLANERY.

SONGS OF THE MONTHS.

_____

TO MARY ELLIOTT FLANERY.

When looking down the vista
   Of long-departed years,
Your eyes may for a moment
   Perhaps be dimmed with tears.

As a longing for the gone-by days
   Of youth fills up your breast;
A longing that cannot be quenched,
   Or wholly be suppressed.

A longing for the heights of fame
   You might have once attained,
For the praise, applause and glory
   You might have sweetly gained.

A longing to rise over
   The sordid, struggling host;
But Fate had destined you, my dear,
   To fill a different post.

Though now you do not longer yearn
   For an illustr'ous name,
For the applause and praise of men,
   For fortune or for fame.
The high position which you fill,
   How few have understood;
Or known its sacred beauty—
   Of wife and motherhood!

And what if household cares may check
   At times the genial flow
Of innate genius in your soul,
   You still take time to sow
Seeds of true love and kindnes
   Wherever you may go.

TO MRS. LOUISA STEELE.

ON RECEIVING SOME SEA-SHELLS.

My sincere thanks to you, dear friend,
For those pretty shells I send;
Tokens they are of friendship true,
So kind and thoughtful 'twas of you
    To send those shells to me.
From where you're now, in perfect ease,
Recovering at Los Angeles;
The needed strength and vigor such
As you, dear, seek and crave so much
    I seem to-day to see!

I see you, when the tide goes out,
Pursuing eagerly the route
That leads you to the sunny beach
Of circling cove and bayland reach,
    Where the great foaming sea
Has lately thrown up with its swell
Flowers, pebbles, moss and shell;
There 'neath fair California's skies
I see your beauty-loving eyes
    With rapid scrutiny.

Selecting rainbowed moonstones bright,
Pink shells and pebbles smooth and white;

I see you watching, day by day,
The ships which safe at anchor lay,
        With curiosity;
Looking upon the ocean grand,
Tracking the white and glist'ning sand,
Gazing with eager, keen delight
After the soaring seagull's flight
        Above the raging sea.

Again my thanks for these, dear friend,
To you with wishes true I send,
That in that land of pleasant clime,
Of never-ceasing summer-time
        And rarest scenery,
Wooded hills, with clustering vine;
Sea-winds, flowers, fruit and wine
Will give you back your needed health,—
Whose worth is more than Fame or wealth—
        'Mid Nature's greenery.

TO MR. AND MRS. G. E. STALEY.

ON THEIR WEDDING DAY.

Since cunning Cupid's mystic darts
Have now united both your hearts,
Accept my wishes, husband, wife,
For a long and prosp'rous life;

As the months and seasons fly,
And the years glide swiftly by,
But rehearsing with each scene
What for ages past has been!

Keep the sunshine, then, I pray,
Ever all along your way;
Be the weather rough or drear,
There's the silver lining clear.

It will make your cares seem lighter,
It will make your joys seem brighter;
Keep it, let it ne'er depart,
Hold the sunshine in your heart.

AN OLD-FASHIONED GARDEN.

Oh, to wander at will in a garden,
   One of my grandmother's day;
One that my grandmother tended,
   Where old-fashioned flowers held sway!

Snowball and flowering almond,
   Zinnias gorgeous in dye;
Lilacs scented and purple
   Which regal robes outvie;

Great silky, blood-red poppies,
   Phlox and sweet-william galore;
Morning glories and holly hocks lusty
   In those happy days of yore,

Blossomed profusely and sweetly
   In splendor and showy array,
But most of those old-time beauties
   Are not in favor to-day!

DAISIES.

Down on the hill on grandfather's farm,
Down on the hill in the sunshine warm,
Beautiful daisies, spotless and bright,
Have expanded their petals, so snowy white.
Oh, daisies, beautiful daisies,
Oh, daisies, in snowy array,
Sweet memories of my childhood
You bring to me to-day.

Down on the hill, oh, daisies white,
've gathered your blossoms in childish delight;
Woven them into wreaths and bouquets
In those happy bygone days.
Oh, daisies, beautiful daisies,
Oh, daisies, in snowy array,
Sweet memories of my childhood
You bring to me to-day.

Were I a child again, happy and gay,
Were I a child again, just for to-day;
I'd be rollicking 'round in the sunshine warm
Plucking the daisies on grandfather's farm!
Oh, daisies, beautiful daisies,
Oh, daisies, in snowy array,
Sweet memories of my childhood
You bring to me to-day.

WHEN DAISIES BLOOM.

Yon field is white with daisies
   As we stand together here;
Sad good-byes fondly breathing
   Sweetheart mine and sweetheart dear!
Striving hard (in soft appeal)
Love's emotions to conceal;
But when daisies bloom again,
We will meet, my sweetheart, then.

ONCE ON A TIME.

Once on a time, no matter when,
   I thought I'd be a rhymer;
A poet that the world would praise,
   No common jingle chimer!

I thought the praise of men would give
   Contentment, rest and peace,
And even riches, too, I thought
   And all my cares release.

And so with eagerness I sought
   The Muse in woodland shades;
In sun and shadowed checkered dells
   And flower-scented glades.

I stood beside clear, limpid streams,
   And on the restless sea
I gazed, but ah, no Muse was there,
   Leastwise not there for me.

And so I wandered back again,
   Back to my own hearthstone;
By Muse of poesy unfired,
   But by experience grown.

Not always the goal we climb for
　　Is it possible to attain,
Not always the thing we wish for
　　Are we able to obtain.

The heights that famous men have reached
　　We all may hope to reach;
But often the striving for them
　　Will a noble lesson teach.

We all were made for some purpose,
　　For a noble purpose, too;
But deeds that the world considers great
　　May not be ours to do.

Then let us ever strive to be
　　Contented with our state;
Nor think that our enjoyment lies
　　Alone in being great.

THOU WILT KEEP THEM.

Thou in perfect peace will keep them,
  They whose minds on thee are stayed;
Though the evil one may tempt them,
  They shall still be unafraid.

Clouds may lower and darkness gather,
  Billows furiously may roll;
Need we trouble when our Father
  Speakest peace unto the soul.

Peace without one ray of terror,
  Peace that comforts day by day;
Peace that passeth understanding,
  May it keep our hearts alway!

JANUARY.

Beneath the leaden skies
Old Mother Earth now lies
   Wrapped in a cloud of white;
Trees once clothed in hosts
Of leaves, now stand like ghosts:
   Each one in snow bedight.

On the ice, smooth and glassy,
The merry lad and lassie
   Are skating to and fro;
Or down the steep hillside
With sleds they gaily glide
   Over the smooth white snow.

The little snow-birds brown—
Feathered warblers of renown—
   So blithe and bright and gay;
Flit about merrily,
Twittering loud and cheerily
   All the livelong day.

FEBRUARY.

Cold now is the breezes' breath
  Covered is the ground with snow;
And in maple forests
  Sugar campfires glow.

Like jewels from trees and cliffs
  Icicles hang a-glittering,
And the little snow-birds are
  Merrily a-twittering.

Above the earth so brown and cold,
  And 'bove the snow so white,
The crocus now opens
  Their golden petals bright.

Cold and windy February,
  We're glad that you are here;
For you bring Valentine Day,
  We love so well and dear.

MARCH.

Hail! gruff messenger of Spring!
March so mad and blustering
With your howling winds that blow
Into drift-heaps huge the snow.

But when there come your latter days
The sap in trees begins to raise,
And far beneath the sleet and snow
Flowers too begin to grow.

What care we for your sleet and snow,
Or how your winds may rage and blow?
For winter now is in its wane,
And 'twill soon be Spring again.

Yes, the Spring is almost here,
And the grass will soon appear,
And the flowers will come again
Beautifying hill and plain.

APRIL.

Beautiful April! sweet month of the Spring!
Mirth, joy and sunshine with thee thou dost bring;
Garlands of bright and beautiful flowers,
Gentle, cool, pleasant, refreshing showers,
And the budding woods with bird-music ring.

The brooklet which so long has been icebound
Now ripples a gentle, musical sound;
From hillsides the snow has melted away
Where the bluebird now sings his roundelay,
And where violets and daisies surround.

Blithe swallows flit and dart through the barn;
Lithe lambkins play in the sunshine warm;
Every creature and thing seems glad and new;
The days they are growing longer, too,
And seed-time again has returned on the farm.

But April! O April! why are you, dear,
So changeful, capricious, and so queer?
Now you bring a hurried shower of rain,
Next moment the sun is shining again,—
First a smile, then a frown, and next a tear.

MAY.

Beautiful Queen of all the Twelve,
　Sweet and bounteous May!
Earth, air and water teem with life,
　All nature is glad and gay.

The Earth in vendure now is clothed,
　Apple trees are in bloom;
On the woodland air the violet,
　Sends forth its sweet perfume.

Among the blooming elders where
　The brook and streamlet flow,
There pout the dainty blue flags and
　Shy night primroses grow.

Down in the green, grassy meadow,
　A-blooming side by side,
Cowslips and gaudy dandelions
　Nod with coquettish pride.

The ever busy honey bees
　Make honey hour by hour;
And sipping sweets the butterflies
　Fly 'round from flower to flower.

'Neath the trees the blue sweet-williams
　Are blooming on the hill,
Where late at eve when day is done
　Sings the plaintive whippo'will.

JUNE.

Sunny, balmy June is here,
  Crowned with scented roses bright,
Growing and blooming everywhere,—
  Oh! what a pretty sight!

Back from the South the birds have come,
  Their last year's nests to repair;
And here to have their summer home,
  And again their young to rear.

Out in the long, wide meadow lot,
  Where the bee honey-hunting goes,
A mower, with his sun-browned face,
  The scented clover mows.

And, vieing with the black-birds' lay,
  The farmer boy at morn
Whistles a love-tune, sweet and gay,
  As he plows out the dew-wet corn.

Many things thou bringest, June,
  Many pleasantries and joys:
Vacation days are coming soon,
  For all school-girls and boys.

JULY.

Long and hot days go by,
Fleecy clouds float through the sky;
And anon a gentle breeze
Softly sighs among the trees,
        In July.

Corn is tasseled and "laid by;"
Daisies blossoming waist high;
Haying time is almost past;
Berries ripen thick and fast,
        In July.

And merry birdies soar and fly
Filling the air with melody;
Poppies are aflame with red
In the flower-garden bed,
        In July.

AUGUST.

No breezes stir the foliage
   Of tree or plant;
Only at early morning
   The birds sweet music chant.

Near noontide's heat, the lazy cows
   Stand in the brook knee-deep,
With drowsy and half-shut eyes,
   Cud-chewing, half asleep.

Boys underneath some spreading tree,
   In some cool and shady nook,
Are idly fishing all day long,
   By some lilied pond or brook.

SEPTEMBER.

Summer days an-ending,
  Autumn coming on;
Trees with fruit a-bending
  In orchard and in lawn.

Apples, soft and mellow,
  In the sun to dry,
Pumpkins, striped and yellow,
  Rip'ning in cornfield lie.

The bushy hawthorn's haws
  Shine crimson in the wood;
Plentiful are paw-paws,
  Luscious, sweet and good.

The shiny milk-weeds now
  Unfold their silken hair,
Which flutters white as snow
  In the balmy air.

The tall iron-weeds
  In their purple glory nod;
On hill-side and in meadow
  Blooms the golden-rod.

Vacation days are o'er,
  With all their fun and noise;
Back at school for useful lore
  Are the boys and girls.

Cloudless ever in the sky;
  Hazy day and dewy night;
So September passes by,
  A month of sweet delight.

OCTOBER.

Softly, lightly, leaves flutter down,
Crimson, scarlet, gold and brown;
Fluttering and whirling through the air,
Leaving the branches brown and bare.

Frosty now the mornings grow;
In hedges are sumac berries, I know;
The golden-rod with modest pride
Still beautifies the dusty road-side.

Apples are gathered and stored away
In th' apple-house for a winter day
Potatoes are out and in the cellar,
With the pumpkins bright and yellow.

Now the katydids are calling,
And the nuts are ripe and falling;
Wood-grapes all are ripe and blue,
And persimmons rip'ning too.

And in the stubble field land
Brown and withered shocks of corn stand,
Where crickets chirrup loud and clear,
Telling us that winter's near.

NOVEMBER.

Rainy November is here,
So melancholy and drear;
Saddest month of all the year.

Ceased is all the harvest din,
For the crops are gathered in
Barn and cellar, crib and bin.

Shorter too the days have grown;
The feathered songsters all have flown
To a warmer, milder zone.

In the woodland dells and on
Hill-side, meadow, field and lawn,
Flowers have withered, all, and gone.

Naked too the trees appear,
Meadow-land is brown and sere.
Old and faded is the year.

DECEMBER.

Winter now has fully come
   With its heavy frost and snow;
Frozen over is the brooklet,
   Ceased now is its rippling flow.

All the pretty little flowers
   That went to sleep so long ago,
Are snugly covered over
   With the pretty, shielding snow.

But the outside is forgot,
   By the cheerful hearth-fire's light,
Where merry games are going on
   'Mong the group so gay and bright.

Snowy, icy, cold December,
   Oh, how much we love you, dear,
For you bring dear Christmas with you,
   Merriest day of all the year.

MUSINGS ON THE OLD YEAR.

Another year has rolled away,
   Forever past,
Forever gone;
   Oh! how fast
Time moves on,
Speeding, speeding ever away.

Oh, how, oh, how, have I spent all
   The bygone year?
Alas! have I
   Caused one tear
From the eye
Of some loving friend to fall?

Would to-day I could recall
   All of the past
Wrongs I have done
   In the last
Year that's gone,
And from memory's page blot out them all.

BEAUTIFUL SNOW.

Beautiful snow, so pure and white,
   Dancing through the air you go;
Falling so gently, softly and light
   From th' clouds above to the earth below.

Beautiful snow, so pure and white,
   Th' crowning beauty of winter cold;
Falling both by day and by night,
   Falling on mountain-top and wold.

Beautiful snow, so pure and white,
   Falling gently on vale and dell;
Cov'ring the cottage of the poor,
   And the mansion of the rich as well.

Beautiful snow, so pure and white,
   Falling on things both high and low;
Hiding the fallen leaves out of sight,
   While o'er the brown tree you thickly blow.

Beautiful snow, white and pure,
   Oh, how I love to see you fall!
Oh, I am certain, yes, I am sure,
   Nothing's as pretty as snow at all.

Lord! make my heart as pure and white
   As the snow when it falls from above;
Fill me with Thy truth and light
   And sweet, beautiful faith and love.

A SIGN OF SPRING.

As I was walking in mid March
  By a flowing brooklet's side,
Half hid in the brown dead leaves
  One little blossom I spied.

There was snow upon the ground,
  And some ice was in the brook;
But this flower was blooming sweetly
  In an icy, shaded nook.

And there was not, no, there was not,
  Anywhere else to be seen
Another blossom, not even
  One single sprig of fresh green.

Well, I'll tell you, for I'm thinking
  That you really want to know
What flower it was, that struggled
  'Gainst wintry sleet and snow.

'Twas just an hepatica,
  Faintly tinged with pink,
And I'm going to tell about it,
  Just exactly what I think;

That it must have clean forgotten
  That the weather was so cold,
Ere its little velvet petals
  It shyly tried to unfold.

Or perhaps it bloomed on purpose
  To tell me Spring was near;
And it may be,—yes, I'm certain—
  Early Spring's already here!

SPRING AGAIN.

Spring, with all her splendor,
  With all her merry train,
Her birds, her flowers, her sunshine,
  Has returned to us again.

On lowly, sloping valleys
  The plowman turns the sod;
Th' dogwood, white with blossoms, gleams
  Beside the golden-rod.

Th' sheep and cattle, peaceful,
  On hill-side pastures stray,
Where spring the dandelions.
  And buttercups so gay.

Th' martins, back from Southland
  Have nested near the door;
The song of happy bluebirds
  Now rings the forest o'er.

EASTER.

TO SISTER.

Oh, joyful, glad Easter morning,
 When Jesus arose from the tomb!
Whose radiant light and beauty
 Dispelled the darkness and gloom.

The ugly and brown bulb-lily,
 Which with care we buried last fall,
In the fertile soil of our door-yard,
 Does the Resurrection recall.

We buried it, full believing
 'Twould appear again in the spring,
With green leaves and snow-white blossoms—
 A lovely and beautiful thing.

So, with equal faith, our dear ones
 In the cold ground we lay away;
We think that they, like the lily,
 Will appear again some day.

The promise to Martha given,—
 "Thy brother shall rise again,"—
Is ours, and firmly we grasp it,
 Steadfastly hope, nor complain.

When our near and dear and loved ones
  We bury from sight away,
We hope, we know, they shall rise again
  On the Resurrection Day.

EASTER LILIES.

O, lovely Easter lilies
  Perfumed with fragrance rare;
O, lilies pure and spotless,
  O, lilies sweet and fair!

O, splendid Easter lilies,
  What is your mission, say?
What message do you bring me
  On this glad Easter day?

O, pretty, snow-white lilies,
  This Easter morn you bring
A message from my Saviour,
  A message from my King.

O, perfect Easter lilies,
  A lesson unto me
You've taught, this Easter morning,
  Of spotless purity!

DECORATION DAY.

Scatter flowers o'er the graves
Where sleep our dear and honored braves;
Bring those emblems of love to-day,
Flowers, so pure, beauteous and gay:
Scatter them, scatter them o'er.

Strew them lovingly over all,
Caring not on which ones they fall;
On the grave of the hero-lover,
Husband, father, son and brother:
Strew them lovingly o'er.

And cover them careful over,
Cover the grass and running clover;
Cut down the briers and weeds that are there.
And cover their graves with blossoms fair:
Cover them carefully o'er.

Lay them gently o'er, bouquet and wreath,
Think of the heroes lying beneath;
Some who bravely fought and fell,
Nobly dying by bullet and shell:
Lay them gently o'er.

Tenderly o'er their ashes, dear,
Place blossoms, and moisten them with a tear;
Naught our love for those brave shall blight,
WWho died for freedom, peace and right:—
Place them tenderly o'er.

Shower them over, freely shower,
Beautiful, bright-colored flowers;
While the loved old "red, white and blue,"
Floats o'er our living veterans few:
Shower them freely o'er.

Heap them o'er, lavishly heap
Violets, pinks and pansies deep;
Roses redder than sunset's glow,
And lilies pure and white as snow:
Heap them lavishly o'er.

Yes, where our heroes dreamless sleep,
And 'bove them clover and myrtle creep;
Bring those emblems of love to-day,
Flowers so pure, pretty and gay;
Scatter them, scatter them o'er.

THE SWORD IN ITS SCABBARD.

The sword is sheathed in its scabbard,
  The muskets are stacked away;
The cannons are silent and rusted,
  And going to decay.

Our battle-field deserted,
  Where Spring rains gently fall,
We hear no more the drum-beat,
  Nor bugles sum'ning call.

The grass is growing verdant,
  Over the many graves
Of heroes brave, who fought to free
  The toiling, suff'ring slaves.

How many, oh, how many,
  Enlisted in the strife!
Youths into manhood budding,
  And men in the prime of life.

Youths whose noble ambitions
  And hopes were laid aside;
All for love of their country,
  For which many bled and died.

Men who left behind them
　　Wives and children, and all
That were near and dear and precious,
　　And went at their country's call.

God bless our dear dead soldiers!
　　God bless the living ones, too;
Our nation will ever honor
　　And cherish such heroes true.

MEMORIAL DAY.

They are not dead! They are not dead!
  Those soldiers true and brave;
The heroes who suffered, fought and bled,
  Our country dear to save.

Their names are in the Book of Life
  Their battles all are o'er;
All their heart-burnings, pains and strifes
  Have ceased forevermore.

They all are living now above,
  Tho' their ashes here may be;
And inspire us still with fervent love
  For home and liberty.

They all are living, and they see,
  (Tho' invisible are they)
Our country prosperous and free,
  On this Memorial Day.

BERRYING TIME.

Heigh-ho! for the fields and meadows,
  And the walls and hedges high,
Where in plenty grow the berries
  That ripen in July.

See the little boys and little girls,
  Full of noise and fun;
With broad-brimmed straw hats and bonnets
  To shade them from the sun.

Merry, happy, gay and cheerful,
  With bucket, cups and pails,
They are trudging over hill-sides,
  And through the grassy dales;

And by old walls and hedges,
  Along the hot road-side,
In hollows near th' forest's edge,
  And 'cross the pastures wide;

By old, deserted cabins,
  And by the water-mill,
They go in search of berries,
  Their cups and pails to fill.

God bless the happy children,
  Now they are coming back,—
All their pails and buckets laden
  With berries sweet and black.

Then heigh-ho! for the fields and meadows,
  And the walls and hedges high,
Where in plenty grow the berries,
  That ripen in July.

AN AUGUST SUNSET.

With what a glory in the west
Sinks the golden sun to rest!
Sinks he from our sight away,
Sinks he at the close of day.

Oh, what colors beautify
The refulgent western sky,
'Cross which streaks of purple, red,
Pink and amethyst are spread.

Adown the mountain-slopes, pure streams
Of lovely, golden sun-light gleams,
And shines so bright, and sparkles and
Dances so beautiful and grand.

In yon crystal pond, reminding me
Of that heavenly, glassy sea,
Mingled with fire, lovely, sublime,
Of which I've read from time to time.

So doth the great sun sink away
Calmly at the close of day,
In splendor which by far outvies
That splendor showing at its rise.

As calm, as lovely and serene
Is one whose life has useful been;
More beautiful in its closing hour
Than in the first flush of its power.

A GOOD-BYE.

It was only three days ago,
  I sadly said good-bye
To all my pretty flowers, and wept
  To think that they must die.

To my beautiful tea-rose
  Which by my window stood;
Which then was full of blossoms
  And tender shoots and bud.

And to my scarlet-flowering sage,
  And petunias red and white,
My zinnias and my dahlias,
  And yellow 'sturtiums bright.

I said good-bye with tear-dimmed eyes,
  For were not these the flowers
Which to me had been comrades
  Through by-gone summer hours?

My lovely loved chrysanthemums,
  (My pride and my delight)
Which bloomed along my garden path
  In colors gay and bright.

And my purple cosmos, lately bloomed,
　Tho' not loved any less
Than those that bloomed all summer long
　In constant loveliness.

And yet I said good-bye to all,
　For winter hastens fast,
And I knew full well their beauty
　Could not forever last.

NUTTING-TIME.

When the nights have lengthened,
　　And the days have shorter grown;
When the birds have flown southward
　　To a milder, warmer zone;

When the nights and mornings have
　　Grown frosty, sharp and cold;
When leaves have changed their color
　　From green to red and gold;

When apple trees are burdened
　　With delicious apples bright;
When the creseent harvest moon
　　Shines all through the night,

Then to hunt and gather nuts,
　　What fun and what delight!
And store them away to eat
　　By winter fires bright.

Hickory nuts and walnuts,
　　Hazelnuts and chestnuts brown;
Butternuts and chinquapins,
　　Listen at 'em patter down!

Now and then a squirrel
  Who thinks perhaps he isn't seen,
Frisks quickly o'er the ground,
  With quiet, cautious mien.

Quickly but quietly he gets
  His nuts in innocence;
Then goes a-frisking up the hill,
  Far by the old rail fence.

As if to say, with impudence:
  "If you can, catch me!"
Then disappears among the trees,
  In triumph and in glee.

INDIAN SUMMER.

Ere winter puts his icy mantle on,
   Well trimmed with ice and snow;
For a little season we enjoy
   The loveliness of Indian Summer glow.

Oh! what a lovely season 'tis,
When the sunlight shines dimly through
The almost naked woods!
When the air is hot and hazy, and when
Gentle zephyrs softly blow,
Reminding us of by-gone summer hours.

O, lovely Indian Summer, we
Would fain enjoy your season longer,
Ere the cold and dark and somber days
Of winter come.

A THANKSGIVING.

Dear Lord, we thank Thee for the crops
   Of white and golden grain,
Which now are safely gathered in
   From winter's sleet and rain!

And for the fruits and for the foods
   In cellars stored away;
We thank Thee now, dear blessed Lord,
   On this Thanksgiving Day!

Not only for the crops this year
   (So bounteous and free)
Of grain and fruit so plenteous
   Do we give thanks to Thee;

But for the many gifts which Thou
   Hast on us all bestowed;
Each day, each hour and all the time,
   We thank Thee, blessed Lord!

CHRISTMAS WISHES.

TO A FRIEND.

Many Christmas wishes, friend,
To you on this day I send;
First, I wish your home to be
Filled with cheerfulness and glee;
May your fireside snug be bright
With that gentle, radiant light,
That beautified that holy night
In Bethlehem of yore.

And may gentle love, serene,
Be your law and be your queen;
And may peace and happiness
You and yours forever bless;
And social mirth and gayety,
And all the pleasures that there be
On earth,—I wish them all to thee.
And thine forevermore!

Many welcome gifts, dear friend,
I hope your friends to you may send;
But one gift I hope that thou
Hast possessed long ere now.
That, the gift of love divine,
Fair to-day I hope shall shine
Brighter over thee and thine
Than e'er it did before.

THE HILLS.

He is not destitute of lore,—
   Far, far from it is he,—
Who doth the mighty hills adore,
   And love them reverently.

Methinks they who make their abode
   On plain and valley wide
Are not so near to heaven and God
   As those who by hills abide.

Tho' sweet your city life may be,
   Yet sweeter, sweeter still
Is my quiet country life to me,
   By vale and lofty hill.

Far from the city's strife and care
   I live a life obscure;
I breathe the sweet health-giving ai
   And drink the water pure.

The rugged, rocky peaks I climb,
   Which bold and peerless stand,
Majestic, mighty, huge, sublime,
   So beautiful and grand!

The wondrous works of God I view
  In every dell and nook;
And daily learn some lesson new,
  From Nature's open book.

Here calm and wooded glens afford
  The noblest, purest kind
Of inspiration for the bard's
  Dreamy and gifted mind.

And here is music never still,
  Not tiresome, weird or dull;
And here are scenes for artist's eye,
  Lovely and beautiful.

How oft their grandeur I've admired
  As 'neath them I have stood;
And it was they that me inspired
  To love the pure and good.

How sweet among their vales to roam,
  And view their summits high;
Here may I ever have a home,
  Here may I live and die!

THE LONE GRAVE ON THE MOUNTAIN.*

Upon a dreary mountain top
　　Where pine trees dismal moan,
There is a solitary grave
　　With briers and weeds o'ergrown.

They say a soldier fills that grave,
　　Who bravely fought and died
For rights and liberties
　　On the Confed'rate side.

But little does it matter now,
　　Can't we forgive his fault?
And the faults of his fellow soldiers
　　As we stand by his wooded vault?

No name is on the rough pine slab
　　Which marks the lonely spot;
　　His name is not forgot.
But in some far-off Southern home

No loving friends nor kindred
　　Have wept here by his grave,
Or planted flowers tender
　　Over his bosom to wave.

---

* Bull Mountain, Floyd County, Kentucky.

They know not where he reposes,
  They cannot find him to-day;
They just know that he died in battle,
  From home and friends far away.

So let us to-day bring flowers,
  And tenderly strew above
The dust of the sleeping soldier
  These tokens of our love!

TO W. A.

There's not a breeze that passes
  But it seems to bring to me
Some tender, looked-for tidings,
  Some message, love, from thee.

There's not a bird that singeth
  From wall or bush or tree,
From roof of vine-wreathed balcony
  But singeth, love, of thee.

There's not a flower that blossoms,
  But your kindly, pensive face,
With loving eyes and heart love
  On its painted leaves I trace.

There's not a stream that murmurs
  Through wood or grassy lea,
Down mountain side or hollow
  But will murmur, love, of thee.

In all of Nature's beauties,
  Whatever they may be;
Where'er they are, it matters not,
  I see and hear of thee!

HOISTING THE FLAG.

Sept. 22, 1898.

We hoisted the beautiful, beautiful flag,
    Our country's flag so bright and gay,
    Over our little log schoolhouse to-day.

For the love which we had for our country,
    Our country so grand and free;
We hoisted the beautiful flag to-day,
    Our emblem of liberty.

We thought, as we looked upon it,
    How oft o'er the battle plain
It had waved victoriously
    Above the thousands slain.

And we thought of the many thousands
    Of patriots and braves
Who fought and fell beneath it,
    Now lying low in their graves.

'Tis no wonder then that we love it,
    Our beautiful flag so bright,
With its crimson stripes and azure field,
    And its stars so pure and white.

May the crimson stripes remind us,
 Over and over again,
Of the blood of heroic patriots,
 Which was spilled on the battle plain!

The beautiful white, the stainless white,
 Means peace and purity;
 And may our lives, like the white of the flag,
 Pure, fleckless, and stainless be.

And as we look at the blue of our flag,
 So like the fair blue skies;
We think of faith and fidelity,
 Which 'twas made to symbolize.

May we ever love our country's flag,
 With its beautiful colors three,
And the glorious Nation it represents,
 United, proud, and free.

So here's three cheers!   All together!
 For our flag, the best in the world,
As it waves above our schoolhouse
 With its silken folds unfurled!

THE WAGON RIDE.

A REAL HAPPENING.

It was on a visit they came,
Four girls from town, (I'll not tell any name)
Out in the country for a merry "spell,"
But how they came, I'm not going to tell.

And when the day they'd almost spent,
Then all their thoughts were homeward bent;
So Sis and I decided to go
And take them "almost" home, you know.

We first proposed to ride horseback,
Then next into a wagon pack;
And to this last we all agreed,
And piled in the wagon grass and weed
To sit on; then we all got in,
And our rough, jolly ride did begin.

Yes, 'twas a jolly wagon-ride,—
None were there but just girls inside
The rough, old jolty wagon-bed,
Just six young girls, as I have said!

Humpty, bumpty, o'er stones we drove,
And anon through a shady grove
Then up the mountain's steep ascent,
Past farm-houses old and quaint.

Thus we merrily jogged along,
Eating apples, and full of songs;
Guessing what our sweethearts would say
If they should meet us upon the way.

Telling jokes and poking fun,
For every one was frolicsome—
'Twas thus we whiled the time away,
And we had a merry ride that day.

THE FARMER'S BOY.

He's up at daybreak in the morning,
   In his uncouth working frock;
Out in the barnyard, blithe and gay,
   Busily feeding the stock.

He plants and hoes and plows out the corn,
   And he reaps the golden wheat;
And he rakes and stacks the scented hay
   In the scorching summer heat.

He harvests the corn in the Autumn,
   And gathers the apples good
From the tall, old trees in the orchard,
   And he chops the winter's wood.

He hunts the squirrel, rabbit and fox
   In the morning bright and soon;
And he hunts the 'coon and the 'possum
   By the gentle light of the moon.

He milks the cows, he fishes and skates,
   He is full of fun and noise;
He goes to school; he courts the girls,
   And romps with the other boys.

His life is as sweet and gay as can be,
As wild as the daisies fair,
As care-free as bluebird's in summer,
And wholesome as mountain air.

EVENING AMONG THE CUMBERLANDS.

Among the rocky Cumberlands
  A summer day is ending;
Th' woodman now with ax on arm
  His homeward way is wending.

The sun is hid from sight, but leaves
  A pleasant afterglow
On western hills, and quietude
  And peace are reigning now.

And from the woodland pasture
  The cattle slowly roam;
I hear the jingle of their bells
  Now on their journey home.

The robin gay has caroled
  His sweet and good-night lay;
And with his mate has gone to sleep,
  Until another day.

The whippo'will so plaintive
  His night song has begun,
And everywhere's the music
  Of insects' ceaseless hum.

And now and then the night-hawk
  With scream so loud and shrill,—
I hear him on some distant peak,
  When all things else are still.

So calmly and so peacefully,
  Just in this charm-full way,
Among the rocky Cumberlands
  Closes a summer day.

HOLLYHOCKS.

J. S.

To-day as I sit by my window
  With an unread book in my hand,
My hollyhocks close by the lattice
  Are beautiful and grand.

I think of an old-time garden,
  No other flowers were there,
Except the hollyhocks growing
  Without tending, thought or care.

They were masses of bloom in summer,
  So beautiful and so high,
And swayed and nodded coyly
  To all the passers-by.

The house that stood in that garden—
  Its keeper is dead and gone!—
But around it still in summer time
  The hollyhocks bloom on.

SOMEBODY'S FATHER.

'Twas after the battle of Gettysburg,
  Closing slowly was the day,
As we were tenderly bearing
  The dead and wounded away.

On the outskirts of the battle-field
  Was the scene pathetic to see;
'Twas a soldier dead, seated on the ground
  With his back against a tree.

In his hand he held some object
  His eyes on it fixed steadfast,—
An object that must have been dear to him,
  That his eyes had looked on last.

As we drew nearer to him we noticed
  'Twas a picture, that was all.
A picture of two sweet children,
  Two children pretty and small.

Man tho' I was, and knowing well
  What the trials of a soldier are,
And used to carnage and bloodshed
  Through those many years of war;

The sight of that man who had feasted
  His eyes on his little dears
While his eyes were dimmed in the death-haze,
  To my softened eyes brought tears.

In our throats we felt lumps gathering
  (There were six of us in the crowd),
And mist was coming before our sight
  As we stood with heads low bowed.

And I thought, as I stood and saw him,
  Of my far-off Northern home,
Where a loving wife watched for me,
  And a baby boy alone.

So we stood and looked at the soldier,
  With the picture gripped in his hand,
And instinctively each other's thoughts
  We seemed to understand.

We dug a grave for the hero
  And calmly we laid him to rest,
With the picture of the children
  Laid lovingly on his breast.

A sad and touching scene it was,
  We spoke not a single word;
No mournful beat of muffled drum,
  No musket shot was heard.

And by his lonely pillow
  I inscribed upon the tree
Where we'd found him: "Somebody's Father,
  July 3, '63."

WASHINGTON.

Great and loved and rev'renced patriot
　Of unstained and immortal fame,
What grateful memories fill our minds
　At just the mention of thy name!

How justly the "Father of his Country,"
　Thou'rt called, thou friend of liberty!
Full of dauntless and fearless courage,
　Unswerving, faithful loyalty.

Thou wast one of the few, great Washington,
　Who dearly loved thy fellow-men.
Thou lived and labored, and bravely fought
　For the freedom we'll ne'er be denied again.

As a fair, unblemished and spotless gem,
　Thy name on earth will ever shine;
And true honor, love and reverence,
　And fame shall evermore be thine.

THE 'POSSUM HUNT.

A TRUE INCIDENT.

Did I ever 'possum hunt?
  Yes, not very long ago;
And did I catch a 'possum?
  Just wait and you shall know!

Six little boys gathered
  In a group at school one day,
Were talking very earnestly,
  And I overheard them say:

"Now wouldn't it be funny,
  And it wouldn't be impolite,
If we could get our teacher
  To 'possum hunt to-night?"

I'd never 'possum hunted,
  But I thought 'twould be real delight,
So with them I agreed to go
  A-hunting, that very night.

Pawpaws then were ripe and good,
  And plentiful as well;
And I'd always heard that 'possums
  Liked them exceeding well.

And knowing this we hit upon,
　　As we thought, a splendid plan
To take some pawpaws, which we thought
　　Would be lots better than

Any dog; and so we did.
　　It was a lovely night;
Everything was calm and still
　　The moon shone clear and bright.

We went about twelve miles—or more—
　　I'm fully satisfied;
Over hills, down rocky creeks,
　　And by the river-side.

But lo. , before we reached our homes
　　The sky was overspread
With dark and threatening rain-clouds:
　　And faster home we sped.

And then, to make the darkness worse,
　　Our very feeble light
Went out, yet we (though tired and scared)
　　Kept on with all our might.

We had thrown away the pawpaws
　　Of which we had a stock;
'And we reached our homes in the morning,
　　At half past three o'clock,

Hungry, tired and sleepy,
　　With bedrabbled shoes and dress;
But did we catch a 'possum?
　　I will leave you that to guess!

THE "EVENING STAR."

TO MOTHER.

When behind the rugged mountains
  The golden sun has gone,
When daylight's splendor fadeth,
  When twilight stealeth on;

I take my seat out on the porch,
  Where happy children are,
And wistfully and sadly view
  The shining "Evening Star."

Tho' the children seem so happy,
  So frolicsome and gay,
As on the porch's threshold
  And banisters they play;

Yet my heart grows sad and lonely,
  And tears will fill my eye
As I look out at the "Evening star,"
  And think of days gone by.

A little white-washed farmhouse
  Comes this evening to my mind,
Around whose narrow, simple porch,
  The morning-glories twined.

How often on that tiny porch
    I've seated been, with one
I loved so well, at evening,
    When the day's work was done.

Yes, there we'd sit together
    In the twilight gray,
And view with admiration
    The "Evening star's" bright ray.

Oh! that little, narrow, vine-wreathed porch!
    I can shut my eyes, and see
Where I have sat so often,
    My mother dear with me.

How, oh how, I'd love this evening
    To sit with you, mother, dear,
As I used to on that little porch,
    And watch the "Evening star."

(The above poem was written during a fit of
homesickness while teaching a district school away
from home.)

COUNTRY COURTSHIP.

I gazed on a beautiful picture
  That adorned my friend's rude wall,
Not after Michael Angelo's painting,
  Nor Titian,—not at all.

A sketch from some humble artist,
  A bit of landscape view,
Of lovely rural scenery,—
  Perhaps you have seen it, too.

The scene was not uncommon,
  'Twas neither ancient nor rare,
The colorings were not gorgeous,
  Though penciled with every care.

It told the old, old story,
  Of "love's young happy dream,"
The artist's favorite study,
  And the poet's fav'rite theme.

With cap pushed back from his forehead,
  A handsome youth, slim and tall,
In a broad pasture field is leaning
  Over a well's high wall.

A neighboring girl stands by him,
    Modest, shy and sweet;
Underneath her short petticoat, showing
    A pair of pretty, bare feet.

The cows from the trough that are drinking,
    And the blue-bird just above,
Were all that heard what these two said,
    Thrilled with young dreams of love.

RAIN IN THE NIGHT.

Rain in the night is falling
   Softly and gently down,
Pattering on the shingles
   Of the farmhouse old and brown.

And tho' I cannot see it,
   Nor feel its crystal drops,
Yet I hear its constant music
   Upon the old housetop.

Pitter, patter, patter, pit!
   How melodious its sound,
As it trickles from the eave-sides
   And splashes on the ground.

But a feeling so sad, so dreary,
   Which I cannot explain,
Comes o'er me when, at night, I hear
   The pattering of the rain.

AT THE CLOSE OF SCHOOL.

As to-day I sit and muse
   O'er the dreamy past,
In my memory comes a scene
   Of December last.

How well do I remember
   The mountains huge and tall,
That stood on both the sides and rear
   Of the school house quaint and small.

'Twas the last day of the term—
   The teacher was my brother,
And among the crowd that day
   There still was another.

Who comes so vividly just now
   In my fond recollection,
Who had my warmest friendship and
   My dearest, best affection.

Ah! well do I remember,
   Nor shall I soon forget,
His jetty curls and lovely eyes,
   The first day that we met.

Many of the ones I saw,
   Only last December,
At the closing of the school,
   I cannot now remember.

But there is one, yes, there is one,
   Do what I may, go where I will,
His lovely eyes and jetty curls
   Will haunt in my memory still.

SMILE AND SPEAK KINDLY.

Smile and speak kindly, dear brother,
　　Oh! how much there is in a smile,
And a word kindly said to another!—
　　Then smile and speak kindly to all.

To the poor smile and speak kindly,
　　And think it not a disgrace;
A cheery good eve, or good morning,
　　May bring a smile to their face.

Some heart whose love chords are broken,
　　Which your harsh words once thrilled with pain,
A smile and a word kindly spoken,
　　May win back their friendship again!

BRIDAL BLOSSOMS.

M. M.

Standing by the bridegroom's side,
With a sweet and modest pride,
See the fair and blushing bride.

In her curly hazel hair,
And on her bosom, does she wear
Snowy blossoms sweet and fair.

Oh, so wondrous pure and white,
Soft and lovely as the light
Of a summer morning bright!

Lovely blossoms, yet not gay,
Oh, what is their meaning, say?
Emblems sweet, of what, are they?

Why does blushing bride to-night
In the gentle, soft lamp-light,
Wear those pretty blossoms white?

Snow-white bridal blossoms, you
Have a meaning sure and true,
Which till now I never knew.

Are you not the emblem of
Pure and sweet and perfect love,
Likened unto that above?

Lovely bride, as pure and fair
As those blossoms which you wear
In your curly hazel hair.

As the days and years go by
Still I pray, oh, still defy
All that taints thy purity.

DESPONDENCY.

What hast thou done that makes thee despondent?
   Why so downhearted and sad?
Life is too short to be wasted in weeping,
   Why not be cheerful and glad?

Don't stand out in the darkness despairing,
   When there is plenty of light;
"Every cloud has a silver lining,"
   Look on the side that's bright!

Don't think because the day's dark and dreary,
   And constantly falls the rain,
And because the sun is not now shining,
   That it ne'er will shine again.

SAFE AT HOME.

IN MEMORY OF MRS. MINNIE KENDRICK.

Dead! How can I say
  That word of such an one
As Minnie was, whose influence
  Still lives tho' she is gone;
Yes, she is dead; but only passed
  From death to endless life;
Passed away from earthly things,
  Away from its sin and strife,
Away from its sorrow and pain,
  Away from its toil and care,
Only passed from earth to heaven,
  To that home "over there."
Over there, now happy
  With Jesus' blessed own,
On that shining, golden shore,
  Minnie is safe at home.

She had such childish purity,
  And such sweet womanly grace;
O, how we miss her presence,
Her beautiful, smiling face.
To every good cause she was
  An ever faithful friend.
Ready always unto the poor
  A helping hand to lend;

Ready to give a cheery
  Comforting word to the sad,
Ready to help bear their burdens,
  Ready to make them glad.
Tho' we see her no more on earth
  Where she was loved and known,
Oh, the sweet and full assurance,
  To know she is safe at home.

Safe at home with Jesus now,
  Minnie, we know you are,
Where nothing that is sinful
  Your happiness can mar;
Living and enjoying
  That never-ending rest
That remains alone to the people of God,
  The sanctified and blest.
And such you were, dear Minnie,
  Before you went away
To that shining, golden shore
  Of everlasting day;
Where you are waiting and watching
  For your friends and kindred to come,
To ever, ever be with you
  Safe in that beautiful home.

BRING THEM BACK.

How many are out of the fold to-day
How many have gone from Jesus away,
O, how many have wandered astray,
Out of the straight and narrow array,
Foll'wer of Jesus, bring them back
To the straight and narrow track.

Tenderly beckon and gently entreat,
Poor wanderers back to the Master's feet,
And tell them He will not repentance spurn,
Tell them He's anxious for their return,
Sweetly tell them to come back
To the straight and narrow track.

Tell them to kneel at the cross and pray,
Tell them He will not cast them away;
Tell them He wants them for Him to live,
Tell them He'll all their back-slidings forgive
If they only will come back
To the straight and narrow track.

O, child of God, go and bring them in
From the rough, hard, stony path of sin,
Bring them out of the rain and cold,
Bring them into the Master's warm fold;
Foll'wer of Jesus, bring them back
To the straight and narrow track.

IN THY SECRET PLACE.

He that dwelleth in the secret place of the Most High, shall abide under the shadow of the Almighty.—Psa. 91;1.

In Thy secret place, Most High,
　Let us ever dwell;
Guarded by Thy watchful eye,
　All shall e'er be well.

For when dwelling there, we know
　That we shall abide
Underneath Thy wing's great shade,
　Safely by Thy side.

With Thy wings then cover us
　They shall keep us warm,
And the weather chill and drear
　Never can us harm.

Yea, when comes the raging storm,
　Keep us still with Thee;
Round us put Thy mighty arms,
　And we safe shall be.

THE PREACHER'S WIFE.

DEDICATED TO THE WIVES OF THE ITINERANT
PREACHERS OF THE M. E. CHURCH.

God bless his wife, the preacher's wife,
   Wherever she may be;
A cheerful joy, a comfort and
   A blessing, all is she.

Whether from humble cottage, or
   From mansion great and grand,
Where ease and luxury she left
   To travel o'er the land,

With him, her Christlike husband,
   Who doth labor for the cause,
And faithfully doth bear aloft
   The banner of the Cross.

In village and in town is he,
   And on the hill and plain,
Through forests vast, through swollen streams,
   He goes in sun and rain.

Oft persecuted, oft despised,
   His fare is rough and hard,
But God he seeks to please, not man,
   In God is his reward.

And tho' it may not be the lot
  Of her, the preacher's wife,
To mingle as her husband does
  In ruder ways of life,

But hers it is to visit and
  Cherish the sick and weak;
And nurse them in affliction's hour
  And words of comfort speak.

And other's burdens nobly bear,
  The sorrowing hearts to soothe,
And with affection's loving hand
  The dying pillows smooth;

And in the Sabbath school repeat
  The story's oft been told;
And lovingly and gently lead
  The lambs to Jesus's fold.

What tho' her life may trials have,
  Her pathway checkered be,
Will not a golden crown of life
  Be giv'n to such as she?

Far, far away from childhood's home,
  'Mongst other scenes and skies,
These pure and unfamed women live,
  And for their Master die.

All over our dear land to-day
  Are graves where rest their dust;
With their work done they dreamless wait,
  The Rising of the just.

CLOSER TO THEE.

Closer, closer would I be
Drawn to Jesus, day by day,
Closer drawn to Him, and further
Drawn from sin and self away.
Closer, closer would I be,
Drawn, O Blessed One, to Thee!

Closer, closer would I be,
Closer to the Crucified,
Closer to the blood-stained Cross,
Closer to His bleeding side.
Closer, closer would I be,
Closer, closer, Lord, to Thee!

Closer, closer, closer, Jesus,
Draw me closer, closer still,
I am trusting, fully trusting,
For I know Thou canst and will.
Closer, closer unto Thee,
Blessed Jesus, let me be!

IN MEMORY

OF REV. JESSE BALL, WHO ENTERED THE HEAVENLY
LIFE SEPT. 6, 1898.

When from the shining parapets
　Of mighty Heaven above
God sent the reaping angel,
　Not in anger, but in love,

He said, "I send thee now to earth,
　Go to yon little town,
And there a soul you'll find whose fruit
　Is ripe and bending down.

"Go tell him I've no further need
　For him to stay below;
His work is done, I need him here,
　Go now, right quickly go!"

Yea, straightway from the shining gate,
　The reaping angel went,
And came to earth, and there he reaped
　That soul for which his Master'd sent.

Dear friend, we miss you, oh, how much
　We miss your gentle voice,
Whose words were always soft and sweet,
　And made our hearts rejoice.

Poor you were in this world's goods,
    No mansion grand you had;
Your food wa   'ways scant and poor,
    And your b. ly meanly clad.

Tho' old in years, and frail in health,
    You had grown while here, dear friend,
Yet as a faithful man of God,
    Your duty you did to the end.

SHINING FOR JESUS.

Brother, do you shine for Jesus,
    Is your life a life of light;
Always radiant and brilliant,
    Ever shining clear and bright?

Say, oh, brother, are you shining,
    Any time and anywhere,
Every day and every night,
    Always shining bright and clear?

Do others see your light, dear brother,
    And the good work that you do,
And are they constrained, dear brother,
    To glorify your Father, too?

Does your blessed light, dear brother,
    Ever grow the least bit dim,
Or your love and faith and patience,
    Ever any less in Him?

FOUR-LEAFED CLOVER.

IN MEMORY OF MY AUNT, APRIL 21, 1898.

A cherished four-leafed clover
   Lies between
The leaves of my Holy Bible,
   Just as green,

As when dear auntie plucked it
   From the side
Of the garden gravel walk,
   Long and wide.

It was early Autumn, and the
   Nights were chill,
And the corn had commenced rip'ning
   On the hill.

And the leaves to change their color
   Did begin;
For one more gay and showy
   Than the green.

While taking a walk at evening
   Auntie found
This pretty four-leafed clover
   On the ground,

She had walked there oft before,
  So had I,
But had passed it quite unseen
  Unnoticed by.

But now she stooped and plucked it
  From the mass
Of tangled, faded weeds and
  Withered grass.

And in handing me the clover
  Said to take
Them and press them in my Bible
  For her sake.

'Twas the last walk here below
  That she took;
And how well I still remember
  Her fond look.

On that early Autumn evening,
  Which she gave
To me, from eyes, so sunken
  And so grave;

Her thin emaciated
  Hands so pale,
And her slow and trembling
  Step so frail;

And her cough so hollow
  Told too well
That ere long she fair must bid us
  All farewell.

Many, many days and months have
   Passed away,
Passed away and left no traces
   Since that day

Auntie went to live with Jesus,
   Upon high,
Where no sickness ever ent'reth
   Nor any die.

But where every pain and grief
   Is all o'er
And where all are glad and cheerful
   Evermore.

Now each day as I do read
   My Holy Book,
Of the last walk I am thinking
   Auntie took;

And, then saddened, half unconscious,
   Drop a tear
On this clover which has lain
   More'n a year,

Pressed between my Bible leaves
   With such care,
And to me so very precious,
   Lies it there.

SHALL WE KNOW OUR DEAR AND LOVED ONES?

Shall we know our dear and loved ones
　　Who before ourselves have gone
To that fair Celestial City,
　　They whose work on earth is done?

Shall we meet them there in Heaven,
　　Friends to us so near and dear,
Shall we greet them and caress them,
　　As we did when they were here?

Shall, oh, shall we in their company
　　Walk the shining streets of gold,
And behold the city's beauties,
　　Whose half never's yet been told?

Yes, we'll know our dear and loved ones,
　　When to Heaven's streets we go,
And we'll know as we are known,
　　For the Bible tells us so.

Oh, the wondrous bliss of going,
　　To that shining golden shore,
Where our near and dear and loved ones,
　　We shall know forevermore.

"REMEMBER THE MAINE."

Americans, patriotic and true,
"Remember the Maine!"
Which sailed from our own loved coasts away,
On a sunny February day,
Bedecked with "Old Glory" bright and gay.

Americans, patriotic and true,
"Remember the Maine!"
Remember the two hundred and sixty men
Who left on our dear beloved Maine,
And never did return again.

Americans, patriotic and true,
"Remember the Maine!"
Remember the many sad good-byes,
Remember the many weeping eyes,
Remember the many heartaches and sighs.

Americans, patriotic and true,
"Remember the Maine!"
Remember the widows now left alone,
Remember the orphans, too, without home,
Remember the mother bereft of her son.

Americans, patriotic and true,
"Remember the Maine!"
Remember that sad memorial day,
When 'neath the waves of Havana bay
With loved ones aboard she sank away.

Americans, patriotic and true,
"Remember the Maine!"
Remember haughty, heartless and hateful Spain,
Whose treacherous trick caused such endless pain,
Who caused the loss of our dearly loved Maine.

THE CUBAN CAUSE.

What was it caused our nation
    To take up arms 'gainst stubborn Spain?
Was it to only conquer her
    That she might praise and glory gain?

Or was it territorial greed,
    That she might richer be?
Or was it beneficial
    To her on land or sea?

Oh, no, not these, not these at all
    Did ever cause this war;
For it was something nobler
    And holier by far.

It was for suffering Cuba,
    'Twas for her liberty
To save her from the Spanish yoke
    Of awful cruelty.

Who then would dare to say: "Don't go,"
    To relatives or friends,
"And fight for rights and freedom
    'Till Cuba's suffering ends."

RETURN OF OUR SOLDIER BOYS—1899.

They are coming home, they're coming,
   Our soldier boys they are;
They're being mustered out of service,
   They are coming from the war.

Husband, father, son and brother,
   Sweetheart and friend so dear,
All are coming and we'll give them
   A hearty, welcome cheer.

Some are coming from the camp grounds
   In the sunny Southland fair,
Some from Cuba, some from Porto,
   And the Philippines afar.

With what true love and what courage
   They enlisted in the strife;
And the freedom of the Cubans
   Counted dearer than their lives.

And all through the bloody struggle
   They did not "forget the Maine,"
Till they freed the isle of Cuba
   From the tyrant-yoke of Spain.

But now the war is over
    And they're coming home again,
Each one proud he's been a soldier,
    And has helped to conquer Spain.

Tho' some may look pale and sickly,
    And the number fewer be,
Because the graves are thicker
    In Cuba, 'cross the sea,

Yet we'll welcome them more warmly,
    Our boys so grand and true,
As they come marching home again
    In their uniforms of blue.

DECORATION DAY—1899.

I went to the cemetery to-day,
   And saw the little girls in white
Gently strew the soldiers' graves
   With beautiful flowers bright.

I saw old veterans there,
   Old veterans they were,
Who had fought in the early sixties,
   'Neath the red, the white and blue.

And to-day I saw them marching,—
   Those veterans old and gray—
To the music of fife and drum,
   'Round the mounds where dead comrades lay.

Of those "comrades" some had fought
   And fell at Malvern Hill,
At Bull Run and at Antietam,
   And some at Chancellorsville,

And others had fallen at Gettysburg—
   But what does it matter, say,
Whether they died in battle,
   In the thickest of the fray;

Or whether they died of fever
 In hospital tents, alone,
Or after the war was over,
 Surrounded by friends at home?

They were soldiers and we honor them,
 For they did their duty as well
As any of their brave comrades
 Who on the battlefield fell.

I saw to-day young soldiers,
 So very young were some
They did not carry a rifle—
 But carried instead a drum.

Yet noble-hearted and brave,
 And heroic soldiers they are,
They are heroes who enlisted
 In the Spanish-American War.

They were there to do honor and homage
 To their dear, dead comrades, who lay
Peacefully, quietly sleeping
 Beneath new-made mounds of clay.

Their bodies were borne from the battlefields
 Of El Caney and San Juan Hill,
Santiago and La Quasima,
 Where they for their country fell.

We honor the dear, dead heroes
 Of the four years' Civil War,
It was a holy, righteous cause,
 They fought so bravely for.

And we honor those dear, dead heroes,
    Who fought 'gainst stubborn Spain,
To free the starving Cubans
    From slavery's bitter chain.

And to-day we strew with flowers their graves,
    The old ones and the new;
For they're all our heroes, and they fought
    'Neath the old "red, white and blue."

TO ——— ———.

With memory's eyes I see to-day
　That bygone day of long ago,
When side by side and hand in hand,
　And hearts with ardent love aglow,

We strolled adown that country road,
　And felt the gentle evening breeze,
And listened while the blue-birds sang
　Among the wayside beechen trees;

Beneath whose shade awhile we sat
　Where vi'lets white and vi'lets blue
(Emblems so pure of modesty)
　In wild profusion sweetly grew.

Close by those beeches was a spring
　At which you would not let me stoop
To drink from it, but for me made
　Of wahoo leaves a dainty cup.

Life was then to us a joyous psalm,
　A glad, sweet, happy lay:
But somehow things have changed since then:
　We're far apart to-day!

"ONLY A DRUNKARD."

"Only a drunkard!" said my friend,
 As piteous glances I cast
At a bestial form by the roadside,
 While onward we slowly passed.

"Only a drunkard!" yes, 'twas true,
 Only a drunkard was he;
A pitiable burlesque of all that God
 Had created him to be.

His breath came hard and guttural,
 And his reddened eyes were closed;
From between his lips besmeared with dust
 Slime poison slowly oozed.

What heaven-born impulse shall ever light
 Those eyes with rapture and love,
And teach those slobbering lips to sing
 Te Deums with power from above?

And shall lift that soul on wings of fire
 To worship at heaven's shrine;
Shall make him a messenger of God,
 Holy, Christ-like and divine?

And say, has this poor, beastly drunkard
    A mother, a sister or wife,
Who have grieved, and still are grieving
    Over his sad and ruined life?

Say, do the tear-filled wife-eyes,—
    Sad eyes in which the light
Of hope has long been faded away,—
    Do they watch for him to-night?

Ah, yes, there are always eyes to watch,
    And hearts to suffer alway;
Always some woman's tender heart
    To love him from day to day.

For as long as time and sin shall last,
    While pride to shame is akin,
So long shall woman go with man,
    In his revels of shame and sin.

And with her own slender hands shall lift
    His head from the miry clay;
On her own frail shoulders his burden
    Of weakness and misery lay.

Perhaps that face, now so sodden,
    In the bygone days of old
Once peopled her maiden hours with joy,
    With fancies and dreams untold.

That fallen head had a kingly poise,
    Those eyes now bleared and red
Once looked love to her love-bright eyes,—
    But alas, those days have fled!

There was a time when those drooping lips
  Kissed her lips, her cheek, her brow,
Kind words they were only wont to speak,
  But oaths and curses now.

There once were days when those hands, those
      arms,
  (But those days are gone, are dead)
Caressed the delicate form of her,—
  Now they give her blows instead.

"Only a drunkard" to-night he lays,
  A lost ideal he is,
A sad, a wasted, a blighted life,
    And a ruined home is his.

O, the heartaches and the failures
  She suffers every day!
O, the awful shame and misery
  Hid from the world away!

O, woman, divine and heroic,
  So like the ivy vine,
Whose slender tendrils caressful
  'Round the fallen oak entwine.

FUTURE DAYS.

With eager eyes I fondly gaze
Into the dim and future days,
Wondering what's in store for me
In those days that are to be.

What new fields of work shall I
Enter in the by and by?
What new lessons learn, and how?
This I wish I knew just now.

Shall I new friends ever meet
In those days, and fondly greet?
Will they prove as kind and true
As those friends that once I knew?

How will look the dear old home
In the days that are to come;
Will it be as dear alway
To me as it is to-day?

Shall I ever miss the faces,
Miss the loving, kind embraces
Of my father and my mother,
Of my sister and my brother?

Well, those days we cannot know!
And it is best He wills it so;
Enough it is for our ken
What now is and what has been.

THE CORN-HUSKING.

NOVEMBER, 1898.

'Twas a week before Thanksgiving,
  The days were very brief;
The woods were almost naked,
  Save here and there a leaf
Of somber hue was clinging still
  To a tiny, pliant bough,
Which mild October's gentle winds
  Had failed it off to blow.

No flowers shed their fragrance
  On the smoky atmosphere,
For the frost had nipped their beauty,
  And left them dead and sere.
And no little feathered songsters
  Warbled forth their happy lay,
For with the first light snow-fall,
  To the South they flew away.

But on that day of memory
  Of Indian Summer weather,
Within the wide, old shed we sat,
  My love and I together,
With others, husking out the pile
  Of Indian corn so bright
And yellow. How we worked that day,
  From early morn 'till night.

Some talked awhile about the corn,
　　Talked of its size and weight;
How the drought had injured the early,
　　And the rain had ruined the late.
Some talked of preachers, and also
　　How few preached in Jesus' name,
Tho' many preached for money,
　　And many preached for fame.

Some disputed over politics;
　　Some talked of education;
Of men and women teachers
　　From high and lowly station;
Some were too vain and noisy,
　　And some too shy and grave,
Some's manners were too shrinking,
　　And some were far too brave.

But mostly all, both young and old,
　　Talked of the war with Spain;
Of how our gallant soldier boys
　　Had avenged the sunken Maine.
And how Dewey, gallant Dewey!
　　Had at break of day in May
Surprised the Dons, and routed
　　Them from Manila Bay.

And how Lieutenant Hobson
　　Performed his daring feat
When he sank the Merrimac,
　　And stayed Cervera's fleet.
And how, at Santiago hill,
　　The Spanish boys did hustle
When our boys cut the barbed wire fence,
　　And captured Morro Castle.

Well, of course we had a dinner,
　And a sumptuous one at that;
Such as god or epicure
　Would fain have feasted at:
Although it wasn't cooked or fixed,
　In any new-fangled way,
But cooked by good old-fashioned cooks
　In the good old-fashioned way.

But why need I talk so long and much
　Of such a common thing
As a corn-husking which, each Autumn,
　Just thousands of them bring.
Where the huskers all with friendly chat,
　With stories grave and gay,
With frolic, riddle and with song
　While the merry time away.

AFTER THE STORM.

Long ere the sparkling raindrops
    Ceased dripping to the ground
From all the water-laden trees,
    With soft and gentle sound;

The sun in golden splendor
    Shone brightly unawares,
And seemed to turn these raindrops all
    To myriads of stars,

All scintillant with radiance,
    Like Hermon's lavish dews,
Moment'rily displaying
    The rainbow's varied hues.

The birds all fast awakening
    From silent lethargy,
Now trill and warble sweet and clear,
    Their songs o'er wood and lea.

The tinkling of bells is heard,
    As sheep and cattle come
From the hastily-sought shelter
    Before the coming storm;

And wander now about at will
  The hill-side pastures over,
Nibbling drooping daisies
  And luscious grass and clover.

The little, silvery brooklet
  Of just an hour ago,
Is roaring and foaming
  Like a furious, maddened foe.

Now leaping over fallen trees,
  The summer's greenness wearing,
Fence-rails and other débris, o'er
  Its restless bosom bearing.

Yon monstrous, smouldering oak,
  The growth of many a year;
Among the forest trees it stood
  In size without a peer.

Its branches proudly reared aloft,
  But, by one blighting stroke
From heaven, now lies rent in twain,
  A fallen though mighty oak.

Far out in deluged bottom-land
  Are numerous shocks of oat,
Of wheat, of rye, of barley, and
  Just finished haystacks float.

Yon field once gay and beautiful,
  In waving tasseled maize,
Of which the neighboring farmers
  Spoke in their envious praise,

Is now a mass of tangled stalks,
  Of wealth and beauty shorn;
Its once bright, streaming banners
  To shredded ribbons torn.

And here and there the chopping
  Of ax is plainly heard,
Then a dull thud, as fallen trees
  And limbs away are cleared.

Someone's heard driving cattle,
  Then hammering away,—
Telling the tale of fences
  Laid low, and swept away.

But now the sky is clear and gray;
  The moon is shining bright,
Bathing the watery, soggy world
  In silvery rays of light.

The creek has ceased its murmurs,
  All things are calm and still,
Save the frog's sharp croaking,
  Or a cry from "whip-poor-will."

Nature calm, in all her beauty,
  Mockingly smileth on
The devastation she hath wrought,
  Which cannot be undone.

MAPLE LEAVES IN AUTUMN.

Of all the many leaves that change
 Their color in the fall,
The scarlet of the maple
 Is fairest of them all.

The gold of beech and chestnut
 Looks commonplace and dull
When placed beside the maple,—though
 Alone they're beautiful.

E'en the beauty of the oak's leaves,
 By the maples' seem to pale,
Like a weed before the beauty
 Of a "lily of the vale."

O, splendid, gaudy maple leaves!
 When fields are bare and brown,
The hazy days of Autumn with
 A scarlet wreath you crown.

AUTUMN BEAUTIES.

From stubble field, woodland and meadow.
  And roadside I gathered to-day
A basket heaped full of fall beauties:
  Lovely gems of Nature are they.

There are golden-rods, which are so golden
  You'd think they are sure enough gold:
I found them close by the roadside,
  On cliff and on brown barren wold.

There are asters of royal purple,
  With eyes of a bright yellow hue:
And gentians I found by the brook-side,
  Delicate, dainty and blue.

Golden-rods, asters and gentians,
Prolongers of summer are ye;
And to gladden the dull days of autumn,
  Nothing could lovelier be.

THE OLD MILL-POND.

It is evening, quiet evening,
  As I sit before the blaze
Of the hickory fire glowing,
  Musing o'er my childhood days.

Memory, intrusive goddess,
  Gently waves her magic wand
Across my eyes, and I can see
  The old, the old mill-pond.

I am dreaming it is summer,
  I am near my father's home,
I am a happy child again;
  O'er the mill-pond's banks I roam.

O'er its banks with grasses covered,
  Where shines the sunlight bright,
My checkered apron filling
  With blossoms milky white.

Now 'tis summer, and I'm fishing,
  Not for trout, but finny perch;
Or for mussel shells and pebbles
  O'er the sandy bar I search.

Or with feet bared, I am wading
　　Knee-deep in the mill-pond cool;
My mind free from annoying
　　Thoughts of work and books and school.

Autumn: and I'm at the mill-pond;
　　Fishing on its banks I stand,
Or I'm building tiny castles
　　On the moist and yellow sand.

Now 'tis winter; still the mill-pond
　　Is my favorite place to play;
I'm gliding o'er its bosom,
　　Which is frozen now and gray.

Always at the mill-pond with me
　　Was my playmate tried and true;
Staunch friends were we from our childhood—
　　Playmate friend, where now are you?

Dear old mill-pond, dear old playmate,
　　Childhood days so gay and bright;
With that past you all are numbered;
　　Far from me you're all to-night.

THE UNCULTURED MAN.

He does not see nor understand
  The beauty everywhere,
Unveiled by Nature's lavish hands,
  Which cultured minds can see and hear.

He does not see the beauty grand,
  Of towering hills and mountains;
He's heedless to the murmur and
  The gush of brooks and fountains.

He's listless to the songs of birds;
  He does not hear their story
Which cultured ears have daily heard,
  Declaring Nature's glory.

To him no lesson is revealed
  By the flowers' silent preaching;
Not e'en by "lilies of the field,"
  Rich in Scriptural teaching.

The beauteous heavens, star-gemmed,
  The restless, roaring ocean,
With emerald islands diademed;
  Yet no poetic notion

Doth ever in his bosom rise:
　　Nor does he stop to ponder
O'er Nature's many mysteries,
　　Wrapped in deep thought and wonder.

What matter if the western skies
　　With sunset splendors glow?
What matter if the night-wind sighs
　　Plaintively, sad and low?

Sunsets to him merely augur
　　The weather of to-morrow;
The night wind's sigh, no mystic spell
　　Casts over him of sorrow.

He does not meditate and brood
　　O'er things grand and sublime,
When gazing on the budding wood
　　And fields in gay springtime.

Summer, with myriads of flowers
　　Bedecking hill and plain,
And cool, dark, shady, leafy bowers,
　　And fields of waving grain.

Grave Autumn with her mellow haze,
　　Her garnered fruit and grain,
Her sturdy forest trees ablaze
　　With red and yellow leaves.

And Winter, with each brook and pond
　　Spread with a pearly sheet
Of ice, and every tree bough donned
　　In snowy whiteness neat.

They come and go, he heeds them not,
 The beauties of each season;
From them no lesson has he got,
 No lofty thought or reason.

What matter if the earth is fraught
 With poetry and music;
He hears, he sees, he feels it not,
 Nor does he care, poor rustic!

The beauties all about his way,
 He cares not to embrace,
But plods along from day to day,
 All things just commonplace.

A LONGING FOR THE WOODS.

O, to be away, to be away
From the city's crowded streets to-day;
From its hurry, its bustle and din;
Its care and strife and its awful sin.

O, to be in the woodland cool;
O, for a bath in a fern-fringed pool;
O, for the singing of wild-bird sweet,
My tired music-loving ears to greet.

O, for a walk in a grassy dell;
O, for the tinkling sound of bells
Coming from far-off cattle and sheep
A-grazing on hillside pastures steep.

O, for a rest on a dear old stone,
With mosses and lichens over-grown;
With no human presence to intrude,
None to break my silent solitude.

O, for a peep in a darkened glen,
Where the sun's hot rays have never been;
Where the wood-doves softly croon and coo
To their love-mates, the long summer day through.

Where in bright sprays the water falls o'er
A precipice high, barren of roar;
Where wild flowers blow and Dryads dwell:
Sure such a scene has power to quell

This tired feeling of restlessness,
Of sorrow, of pain and wretchedness;
For I'm sick of the city's dust and heat;
I long for the woodland cool and sweet.

THE COLORED SOLDIERS OF THE SPAN-ISH-AMERICAN WAR.

All honor to the colored soldiers,
　Who fought in the Spanish war!
They have certainly shown to the world
　What gallant heroes they are.

'Twas at La Quasima that they
　First showed their pluck and grit;
'Twas there 'mid flying shot and shell,
　They made the Spaniards "git."

Then again they had a chance to show
　Their wondrous fighting skill,
When dauntlessly and bravely
　They charged up San Juan Hill.

O, I tell you it was wonderful!
　It certainly was grand!
The way our colored soldiers fought
　In far-off Cuba-land.

And they never shirked their duty once,
　But did it and did it well,
Tho' many brave ones lost their lives
　As they daily fought through hell.

I think they're the ideal soldiers,
   Tho' a little bit rough and tough ;
Yet they've certainly shown to the world
   They're made of the "proper stuff."

"HER HOPES LIE BURIED WITH HER HERO DEAD."

"Her hopes lie buried with her hero dead."
These were the words which a speaker said
Yesterday, as he gazed o'er the graves
Which held the dust of our hero braves.

He was speaking of her, the youthful maid,
While those newly-made mounds he surveyed;
She it was whose earthly hopes had fled;
Lost and buried with her hero dead.

She was thinking when he'd be her own,
Would be hers and only hers alone,
When their lives would be blended in one:
Ah! blooming hopes which fate has undone!

For when the call for volunteers went
Over the land, by the president sent,
To the island of Cuba to go,
And there Spanish misrule overthrow;

Her lover was one who volunteered.
Thought not of the awful fever; feared
He not the guns of the angry foe;
He was a patriot, a true hero.

Well, he went, and after he was gone,
Still she bravely, but vainly, hoped on:
She looked for him home one day; instead
Came the sad, sad news that he was dead.

How did he die? "In a bloody fight
While gallantly striving to gain the height
Of San Juan Hill, he was a hero true.
Why, a braver man I never knew!"

"And yesterday he got a promote."
'Twas thus his tent-mate and comrade wrote
Who could guess what grief and pain was hers,
And anguish, when this reached her ears.

Too deep and too bitter it was for tears,
And which shall last through the flight of years,
Yes, a grief which time cannot undo:
Ah! why, why, is it such things are true?

But not where he fell, on Cuba's clay,
Not there, but here is his grave to-day,
Which with flowers her loving hands strew
Each year as the seasons come and go.

And to-day, as over his grave she kneels,
A new-born weight of sorrow she feels;
How cruel, cruel is war, she thinks,
As her cup of sorrow and grief she drinks.

She has placed above his sleeping dust
A beautiful anchor of hope and trust,
Woven of lilies and heliotropes;—
But it does not tell of earthly hopes.

Ah, no! For all these hopes took their flight
The day she heard from that awful fight
For humanity, on San Juan Hill,
Where he so gallantly fought and fell.

This anchor tells of her steadfast hope,
A hope which in darkness does not grope;
'Tis a hope that they will part no more
When they meet again on the other shore.

Oh, how many, how many like her
Mourn the loss of a soldier hero dear!
Sadly and alone the world they tread;
"Their hopes lie buried with their heroes dead."

NO SOLITUDE IN NATURE.

Nature has no solitude
  For those who list to her,
Her voice is daily heard to speak
  To them distinct and clear.

Think'st thou the broad expanse
  Of lake, of ocean grand,
The flow of brooks and rivers,
  And stretch of level land,

The grandeur of the mountains,
  The flowers, the grass, the trees,
The rocks, the birds, the insects,—
  Think'st thou not that these,

These things and others, too, which make
  Up Nature, truly they
Speak to the inward man—the soul—
  In accents clear each day.

For are they not the oracles
  Of their Creator; say,
Does he not plainly speak through them?
  Yes, this is God's own way!

For oh, how many souls have first
  Known His rare love divine;
Been lifted far 'bove sin's deep pit,
  Prostrate at Nature's shrine.

Ah, yes, dear Father! yes, how oft
  Thy love our spirits move,
So manifested in our works
  It moves us Thee to love.

JONQUILS.

As I look at you, beautiful jonquils,
　What pleasant memories come
To me, of an early spring day,
　Of my brother and of home.

Yes, 'twas an early spring day;
　The sun shone bright and clear,
The birds were singing, singing—
　Were singing everywhere.

Rejoicing seemed all Nature.
　'Neath heaven's azure dome,
And my darling soldier brother
　From the war was coming home.

I knew that he was coming,
　Was coming on that day;
Was not coming on a furlough,
　But was coming home to stay.

For the war with Spain was over,
　Avenged had been the Maine,
Cuba had gained her freedom,
　Peace was restored again.

I had gathered beautiful jonquils;
　Had gathered them just for him,
My brother,—and carefully placed them
　In the parlor so neat and trim.

And when he came how he praised them,
　Just as I knew he would do,
Because 'twas I who had brought them,
　And 'cause they in our garden grew.

I love you, beautiful jonquils,
　Not only because you are fair,
But you make me think of my mountain home,
　And my brother now 'biding there.

APPLE SAUCE AND CHICKEN FRIED.

You may talk about the knowledge
  Which our farmers' girls have gained
From cooking-schools and cook-books,
  (Where all modern cooks are trained) ;
But I would rather know just how,
  (Though vainly I have tried)
To prepare, as mother used to,
  Apple sauce and chicken fried.

Our modern cooks know how to fix
  Their dainty dishes rare,
But, friend, just let me tell you what!—
  None of them can compare
With what my mother used to fix,
  And for which I've often cried,
When I was but a little tot,—
  Apple sauce and chicken fried.

Chicken a la Française,
  And also fricassee,
Served with some new fangled sauce
  Is plenty good for me,
Till I get to thinking of the home
  Where once I used to 'bide,
And where I used to eat,—um, my !
  Apple sauce and chicken fried.

We always had it once a week,
　　Sometimes we had it twice;
And I have even known the time
　　When we have had it thrice.
Our good, yet jolly pastor,
　　During his circuit's ride
With us once each week gave grateful thanks
　　For apple sauce and chicken fried.

Why, it seems like I can smell it,
　　And even taste it, too,
And see it with my natural eyes,
　　Though of course it can't be true;
And it seems like I'm a child again,
　　Standing by mother's side,
Pulling at her dress and asking
　　For apple sauce and chicken fried.

TO MY LOVE.

Darling, my own dear, ownest love,
　Shall I put on a dress of white,
A red, red rose in my raven hair,
　And meet you at the gate to-night?

By the garden gate that is arched with elms,
　With majestic elms tall,
Where night-birds their sweetest melodies croon,
　And so softly their love-mates call.

Say, darling, will you greet me with a kiss,
　Will you be my love as of yore?
Will you talk of the bliss of our future days,
　And tell me you love me more?

And shall we walk down the garden path,
　Under the sparkling star-lit sky,
While the dew is glittering on the grass,
　And the soft, cooling night winds sigh?

COURTSHIP AMONG THE MOUNTAINS.

Up from the woodland pasture
   Came Farmer Thompson's son,
Driving the cattle homeward
   At the setting of the sun.

The long, narrow, winding pathway
   Was shaded, here and there,
By stately-growing elms,
   And fringed with flowers fair.

Down this narrow, winding pathway,
   In homespun cotton gown,
Came Gracie, the youngest daughter
   Of blacksmith William Brown.

Leisurely she tripped along,
   Her feet were brown and bare;
Over her shoulders fluttered
   Soft braids of auburn hair.

She knew she would meet young Thompson,
   Her lover, on the way,
Driving his cows from the pasture,
   His accustomed duty each day.

But now as she sees him she blushes,
  And suddenly twitches her head,
And nervously fingers her apron
  Of checkered white and red.

But how his eyes beam with love-light,
  As he cries, "Hello! sweetheart Grace!"
And throws his arms about her
  And clasps her in fond embrace.

Onward and down the pathway
  The cattle slowly pass,
Nibbling at blossomed daisies
  And bits of straggling grass.

The golden sun has sunk behind
  The mountains steep and tall;
The moon is shining brightly,
  Twilight is over all.

Among the stately elms
  The night-winds softly sigh—
And still the lovers linger
  Beneath the moonlit sky.

NO ONE LIKE MOTHER.

There is no earthly friend nor kin,
    No, there is no other
Whom we can confidence put in,
    Like mother.
Others may love you for a day,
Soon their love will fade away;
But a mother's love will last for aye.

Others, too, may faithless prove,
    Even your father and brother;
But she, yes, she will always love,—
    Your mother.
Aye! her heart is all aflame
With holy love each day the same,
And pure as crystal drops of rain.

No, there is no earthly friend,
    No, no, not another!
Who will love you to the end,
    Like mother.
She'll help you bear your trials and pains,
Rejoice with you 'midst your joys and gains;
Blest mother-love, it never wanes!

THE SUMMER IS DYING.

The summer is dying, is dying,
  Its splendor is fading away;
And my heart is trying, is trying,
  To still keep cheerful and gay.

As the sun is sinking, sinking,
  Adown the bright western sky,
I can't keep from thinking, from thinking,
  Of the days that have long gone by.

Nor can keep from crying, crying,
  With sad heart and drooping head,
As the wind is sighing, sighing,
  As if for some one dead.

For, oh, it is taking, taking,
  Something out of my heart,
And my heart is breaking, breaking,
  To see the summer depart.

BRYANT.

For him all Nature had a voice,
For him she uttered forth her speech;
And he, like David of old, did each day and night
New lessons from her teachings learn.

All creatures great and small,
The broad and mighty ocean,
Blue lakes and ponds, winding rivers,
Rippling rills and bubbling springs,
And e'en the very ground on which he trod,
Spake inspiration to his noble soul.

The silent solitude of forests,
Its dells and glades, narrow valleys, darkened
By towering cliffs and swaying trees,
Were frequently by him.
Birds, insects, flowers, grass and trees
Were his companions all his life.

AT THE "LOCKS."

ON KENTUCKY RIVER NEAR FRANKFORT.

April 27, 1900. To U. S. S.

The sun shone bright, and the azure blue
Of the sky seemed touching the verdant hue
Of hill-top, wheat-field and meadowland;
A scene that was nothing less than grand,
And one which with pleasure we admired,
(Although from the walk we were somewhat
    tired),
As together we sat on the rough, gray rocks,
Yesterday afternoon at the "Locks."

We watched the river run placid and calm,
'Til it reached the stone and oaken dam,
Then suddenly over with maddening rush,
(Carrying with it the stone and brush)
It splashed and dashed in the water below,
Resembling a bank of new fallen snow;
It splashed and dashed on the walls of rock,
Where the gates of the dam were made to lock.

As over the pond birds flew and played,
You wondered why they were not afraid
Of falling into the water, and too,
You wondered much and wanted to know

If the falls had ever frozen o'er.
You wondered of these and many more,
As together we sat on the rough, gray rocks,
Yesterday afternoon at the "Locks."

AFTER READING THE "SONG OF HIAWATHA."

Bits of Indian superstitions
  My books historical hold,
Fragments of tales and traditions,
  Curious and strange and old.

I had read with awe and terror—
  Those Indian tales so old—
Dull and horrid they seemed; no beauty
  In them could I unfold,

Ere by chance I read the story
  By our own dear poet told,
A story full of traditions,
  An Indian legend old.

Longfellow, our peerless poet,
  Your song's a full translation—
So plain and beautiful—of the
  Historian's dull narration.

Oh, the fascinating beauty,
  Straight from Nature's bounteous fold,
In this tale of Hiawatha,
  In this legend strange and old.

It has brought me near to Nature;
   I gaze o'er her boundless pale
And I see the new-sprung beauties
   In this legendary tale.

I have smelled the breath of forests
   In the springtime of the year,
And the bluebird's song has floated
   From those forests to my ear.

I have heard the rush of rivers,
   Heard the lake's majestic roar,
And on its bosom caught the splashing
   Of Hiawatha's steady oar.

I have seen the smoke arising
   From Hi'watha's wigwam small,
Heard with awe the owl and night-hawk
   Plaintively at night-fall call.

I have seen the broad, dull prairies
   Covered o'er with verdant grass,
Through the somber pines and fir-trees
   I have heard the night-wind pass.

I have heard the panting deer leap
   Wildly 'cross valleys narrow,
Followed close by Hiawatha,
   With bow and sharpened arrow.

And I've seen the setting sun
   Paint the western sky with red;
Seen the moon in yellow beauty
   On the earth her radiance shed.

All of these I've seen and heard,—
   Beauties from Nature's store,
In this tale of Hiawatha;—
   All of these and many more.

I'd not thought such wondrous beauty
   Could be made to be a part
Of an ancient Indian legend,
   Woven in with wondrous art.

More of sunshine than of shadow,
   More of perfect love than hate,
Beauty far exceeds the horrid,
   Beauty, wonderful and great.

Oh, we may from Nature's beauties,
   Where'er they be, thoughts lovely glean,
Though within them yet there may be
   All that's ugly, horrid, mean.

You have taught me this, dear poet,
   You have given all this and more,
Taught me to see with lib'ral eyes
   What I could not see before.

Oh, that we with understanding
   Liberally, unselfishly,
All the beauties, truths and mysteries
   Everywhere about us see.

We would turn our eyes more often
   From the lowly things away,
And our minds from ways of purity
   Would not be so apt to stray.

No, we'd not be pointing always
    At the things uncouth and low,
But the beauties that surround them,
    To understand and know.

We would strive, and, daily striving,
    We would grow more wise and good,
More generous, more unselfish,
    Feasting on Nature's food.

E'en the things we think repulsive,
    The things we can hardly bear,
When with gen'rous eyes we see them,
    A garb of beauty they wear.

TO THE CUMBERLAND MOUNTAINS.

O, Cumberland! O, Cumberland!
  My own dear native hills;
For you, oh, rugged Cumberland,
  With love my bosom thrills.

Your rugged and towering cliffs
  Are beauty and a wonder;
They have withstood for centuries
  The crash of maddened thunder.

Summer finds your craggy peaks
  No caps of whiteness wearing,
From base to crest you greet the eye
  With green majestic bearing.

In childhood's days upon your slopes
  How often have I wandered;
How oft o'er your sublimity
  My childish mind has pondered.

With joy I've plucked the flowers that bloomed
  Within your dells and dales;
With eagerness I've watched the streams
  Plash through your wooded vales.

I've seen within these wooded vales
    The timid, cowering dove;
I've seen the eagle wing his flight
    Your lofty heights above.

Not solely for your beauty,
    Nor because my home is here;
Nor for these dear old mountains,
    In my heart I love you dear.

But within your soil lies buried,
    'Neath a wealth of snow-white flowers,
The only love of my lost youth,
    Of my childhood's bygone hours.

THE OLD WALNUT CRADLE.

Up in the attic I found it,
   Far back in the corner it stood,
Where the sunlight never entered—
   A cradle of walnut wood.

'Twas loaded with castaway rubbish
   Covered with cobwebs and dust,
Abandoned, forsaken and lonely,
   An walnut cradle that must

Have been fashioned by my father
   (But certainly not for show
You would think, could you only see it!)
   More than a century ago.

'Twas rudely made, and unvarnished,
   Yet it served its purpose well;
Eleven babies it's cradled,
   Had it a voice it could tell.

Four sisters and seven brothers,
   And I, the youngest have grown
A tottering woman of eighty,
   And am left alone, alone.

The others have quit their wand'rings,
  They all have "crossed the bar,"
Have met their Pilot, and anchored
  Safe in that Harbor afar.

Oh, this cradle takes me backward,
  I seem to hear it rock
As my mother sits beside it
  In her coarse and home-spun frock.

I can hear her softly singing
  In those happy, golden days,
A lullaby of dreamland,
  While she looks with tender gaze

On her baby's closing eyelids,
  And with earnestness she prays
To her Father up in Heaven
  For her baby's future days.

Oh, form that first bent o'er this cradle,
  Hands that first rocked it to and fro,
Oh, voice that sang and heart that prayed
  In that happy long ago;

How I long, how I wish for you,
  How I long to hear that refrain
Lulling me into dreamland
  Like a careless babe again.

THE KING'S DAUGHTER.

*The king's daughter is all glorious within; her
clothing is of wrought gold.*—PSALMS 45, 13.

No rich and costly gown
   Of brilliant lustre rare,
Woven from Oriental looms;
   No sparkling jewels fair;
No rich and showy laces,
   Nor ribbons she may wear;
No scented, gaudy flowers
   May decorate her hair.

She may not tread in silken hose,
   Nor sit at festal boards
And drink from golden cups, as did
   Belshazzar and his lords.
Splendidly she may not in
   A palace rich reside;
With heraldry she may not in
   A burnished chariot ride.

Yet, she's the daughter of a king,
   A king who's not of earth.
She has that true adorning
   Which is of greatest worth.
"She is all glorious within,"
   Immaculate and whole,
And wrought with gold devoid of dross
   Are the garments of her soul.

AT DANIEL BOONE'S MONUMENT.

IN NATIONAL CEMETERY, FRANKFORT, KY.

And is this stone his monument?
　His ashes lying here?
Immortal, heroic Daniel Boone,
　Kentucky's pioneer?

Has he not o'er these burial grounds
Grim, savage war chiefs faced,
Has he not here the panther fierce,
　The bear and wild deer chased?

Deep in the unbroken forest
　And mountain fastnesses,
And broad and uncleared wilderness,
　Contentment pure was his.

For ordained by Providence he seemed,
　Its instrument to have been
For making Kentucky's wilderness
　A dwelling place for men.

Sleep on, immortal hero!
　Brave, dauntless pioneer;
Kentucky's sons will ever hold
　Your name and memory dear,

While the old Kentucky river,
 Whose tide you've forded oft,
With rippling music sings for you
 A requiem sweet and soft.

TRUE LOVE NEVER DIES.

AUTUMN, 1895.

I loved you, dear, when first we met,
　Almost a year ago.
I loved you then, I love you yet,
　But why I do not know.

We met, we parted, that was all,
　On a sunny, pleasant day,
When the leaves were stripped last Fall,
　Of all their colors gay.

We met as only strangers do,
　With simple courtesy;
I showed no signs that I loved you,
　You none that you loved me.

And yet I love you, I confess
　I love you, dear, and well,
With such a love I can't express,
　Nor half begin to tell.

Some say that love if cherished not
　Will fade away and die.
Ah, one we love can't be forgot,
　True love can never die.

A MEMORY.

We two stood together one day
'Neath the pleasant skies of May,
In the shadow of the locust-trees
Where blew the perfume-laden breeze.

The birds above sang clear and sweet,
The brooklet murmured at our feet,
Reflecting in its waves the hue
Of forests green and heavens blue.

And at our feet the grasses grew;
Among them almost hid from view
Were vi'lets; each with shy, sweet grace,
Had drooped its head to hide its face.

O, violets, that seek the shades,
And zephyrs mild of forest glades,
The solitude of darksome nooks,
And murmurs of clear sylvan brooks!

From crowded ways and crowded walks
And from the gossiper's dull talks
That day we held ourselves apart,
To know more of each other's heart.

And sought like you the forest's shade,
And there our sacred love-vows made;
Trose vows are just as firm to-day
As on that bygone day in May.

I held her dearest hand in mine,
O, small, soft hand, you seemed divine—
And earnestly I gazed into
Her pensive eyes of tender blue.

My heart with new-found love was thrilled,
As her sweet eyes, with tears half-filled,
Spoke truthful love to me far more
Than e'er her lips had spoke before.

Ah, many years ago that's been,
And many summers we have seen
Together, since that day, dear pet,
When 'neath those locust trees we met.

Where you, with sweet, uplifted face,
Wearing the violet's modest grace,
With pure, enraptured love and bliss,
Sealed those sweet love-vows with a kiss.

TO S. E. D.

ON RECEIVING A BOUQUET OF PEONIES.

Thanks, thanks, dear friend, for your present,
    For these peonies three;
This mass of milky petals,
    And your kindly thoughts of me.

I thank you for the memories
    They bring to me to-night,
These flowers beautiful and perfect,—
    These flowers of purest white.

They bring me a breath of country air.
    They whisper of prattling rills,
Of purple skies with sunlit clouds,
    Of wooded, templed hills.

They take me back to my childhood days,
    Days past, long years ago,
To a shady, country door-yard
    Where they were wont to blow.

Then accept my thanks again dear friend,
    For these peonies three,
This mass of milky petals,
    And your kindly thoughts of me.

"YANKEE DOODLE."

[During the charge up San Juan Hill the Sixth
Sixteenth and Seventy-first became somewhat
mixed up, until the Seventy-first took up the song,
"Yankee Doodle," which gave the soldiers new
life. They dashed up the hill through a blinding shower of shot and shell, singing this old national refrain till the coveted block-house was
theirs.—History of Spanish-American War.]

They were singing "Yankee Doodle"
　　In the very mouth of hell,
Where bullets whizzed and cannons belched
　　Their deadly fire of shell.

They sang it with the ardor
　　That General Gates' brave men
Sang it to Burgoyne's army
　　At Saratoga, when

Burgoyne's men—well trained regulars—
　　Had had enough of fight
And mixing-up with Yankees
　　On Saratoga Height.

They sang it while their comrades fell,
 And while their comrades' blood
O'er San Juan's sloping sunlit hill
 Flowed down, a crimson flood.

They sang it, still they sang it
 Until the height they attained;
Till they took the guarded block-house,
 And the victory was gained.

ENSIGN WORTH BAGLEY.

'Twas not in the way he'd hoped for,
  Oh, no, not this did he crave
That his country's love and reverence
  Should only be shown at his grave.

That her people then should call him
  Loyal-hearted and true,
Faithful to his country,
  To her banner of "red, white and blue."

He had hoped through heroic daring
  To reach the heights of glory,
When with honors immaculate his name
  Would live in his country's story.

His name will live while our country lives,
  For who would dare gainsay
That he proved to the world his sterling worth—
  In that fight at Cardenas Bay.

Yes, he has reached the heights of fame,
  And in our hearts to-day
We hold for him a reverence
  That will remain true for aye.

For 'twas no common thing to be
 The hero of a battle;
To die as he died at the front,
 'Mid cannon's roar and rattle.

Nor was it any common thing
 His gallantry to prove,
No easy, common thing to win
 A nation's praise and love.

But it is his, the nation's praise,
 But not with shouts and cheers
Does she applaud his name to-day;—
 She mourns his loss with tears.

THE OLD ATTIC ROOM.

On the roof the rain is falling,
 And with wistful eyes I gaze
Backward to the scenes of childhood,
 Gone by, happy, dreamy days.

I can see the old stone mansion
 With its square built spacious rooms,
And its wide and ample porches
 Twined with honey-suckle blooms.

But my mind is over-shadowed
 With a bit of grief and gloom,
As my fancy takes me onward
 To the low-roofed attic-room.

Barrels full of time-worn papers
 And books in this attic stood,
Trinkets strangely old and curious,
 Filled great chests of cedar wood.

Furniture was there all broken,
 So old-fashioned, strange and queer,
Ruffled, silken petticoats,
 And grotesquely-shaped head-gear.

Among this old and cast-off rubbish
  Lots of fun I oft have seen,
With my brothers, Frank and Willie,
  And my sister Josephine.

Not for all the wealth of Croesus,
  Nor for castle walls of kings
Would I change that low-roofed attic,
  With its queer old-fashioned things.

For a wealth of pure enjoyment
  Round that attic-room was wound,
Which through all the years that followed
  Nowhere in the world I've found.

Brothers, sisters, we are parted,
  From that home we're far away;
With its weather-beaten attic,—
  Ah, we're far from it to-day.

Oft in those days I've mentioned
  'Neath its rafters brown we dwelt,
Where from pelting rain and hail storm
  Safe, securely safe we felt.

SING ME A SONG.

Sing me a song, not of houses and streets,
  Not of stifling, smoky air,
Not of busy, bustling feet,
  Not of turmoil, strife and care.

But sing me a song of meadows green,
  Clad in sunshine's golden light;
Skirted with broad-armed elm trees,
  Studded with daisies white.

Sing me a song of whispering woods,
  Watered by silvery, bubbling brooks;
Of dells so narrow, and valleys dark
  Where violets hide in mossy nooks.

Sing me a song of a lakelet blue,
  Where broad leaved lilies rock and float.
Sing me a song of music sweet,
  Straight from a feathered songster's throat.

Oh, sing me a song and take me there,
  Take me back to those country joys,
Oh, take me away from crowded streets,
  Take me away from the strife and noise.

STORY OF THE CHRIST-CHILD.

Would the muses me inspire,
   I to-day would tell to you
Story old of the Christ-child,
   Dear old story, sweet and true.

How at night the lowly shepherds
   Watched their flocks on Judea's hills,
While the night-wind's music mingled
   With the music of the rills.

I would tell you of the tidings
   Which were borne that night to them,
"Peace on earth, good will to men,
   Christ is born in Bethlehem."

I would tell you how those shepherds,
   In that country far away,
Came to where within a manger
   The sweet little Christ-child lay.

I would tell you how the wise men,
   From the western plains afar,
Guided were into Bethlehem
   By a bright and wondrous star.

I would tell you how they worshipped
　Him the infant Jesus dear,
How they gave him costly presents,
　Gold and frankincense and myrrh.

I would tell you all about it,
　All about this story old,
Of the Christ-child in the Manger,
　Though I know it's oft been told.

But the gift to paint word-pictures
　Suitable for such a birth;
Suitable for One so holy;
　For the Saviour of the earth,

Is denied me. I can only,
　I can only tell you where
You can find this beauteous story—
　In the Bible. Read it there!

MEMORIES OF HOME.

Thoughts of the dear old homestead
   Haunt my memory to-day;
Thoughts of my home, my childhood's home
   Far away, far, far away.

Far away in East Kentucky,
   There beneath her towering hills,
Rich in forestry and beauty,
   Watered well with brooks and rills,

On a farm—the old, old homestead—
   Which to me is still endeared,
I was born a baby tiny,
   And to womanhood was reared.

Lilacs purple, roses yellow,
   Massive blooms of snow-balls white,
Beautiful the ample door-yard
   In the sunny springtime bright.

Woodbines sweet and morning-glories
   Rife with butterflies and bees
Climbed and clambered round the doorway
   In the sunshine and the breeze.

Often rang through that old farm house
  Childish voices gay and sweet;
Oft its walls of log have echoed
  Patter of the childish feet.

Down below the apple orchard
  From a fern-clad mossy bank
Where the naiads love to linger,
  Where the elders, tall and rank,

And the willows cast their shadows,
  Where the night-birds sweetly sing
To the moonlight and the starlight,
  Bubbled forth a sylvan spring.

Oh, my eyes are getting tear-filled,
  As before my memory come
Those scenes of my early childhood
  In my East Kentucky home.

Which is now fore'er deserted
  By my father's bright household;
It has now been changed and altered,
  Into strangers' hands been sold.

Some of that dear homestead's members,
  Many past-gone years have trod
In a far and distant country:
  Others sleep beneath the sod.

O'er the graves of those dear dead ones
  Marked by moss-grown chiseled stone
All the years in wild luxuriance
  Have the grass and flowers grown.

DECATUR'S DARING DEED.

FEBRUARY, 1804.

In the deepening shadows of twilight,
  Disguised in a ship of war
Which had been taken from the enemy,
  Sailed Commodore Decatur.

From Sicily's isle through the salty waves
  Of the Mediterranean Sea,
To perform a deed that would live through time,
  Which on history's page would be

A truth that the heroic young might read,
  Or list to their grandsires tell,
How he and his crew performed their deed,
  How bravely and how well.

How into Tripoli's harbor,
  Unseen and unknown, he dashed,
'Till 'longside the Philadelphia
  The little Intrepid he lashed.

Then aboard the Philadelphia
  He and his brave crew sprang,
While the sound of their guns and the enemy's,
  On the tropical night air rang.

How he left the Philadelphia
  Ablaze in the harbor blue,
After he'd captured and taken aboard
  The survivors of her crew.

Honor to all our heroes
  Who laurels for bravery have won!
But our history records no braver deed
  Than that bv Decatur done.

ANSWER TO VERSES ADDRESSED TO ME BY PETER CLAY.

Backward down the stream of time
  My wandering mind now floats,
When I a hoyden country lass,
  In homespun petticoats

That reached down to my ankles bare,
  Ankles bare and brown, too;
Not browned by summer suns, for birth
  Had giv'n to them that hue.

I think now of those days when hills
  And vales with music rang,
Of which in crude, uneven,
  Yet rhythmic, words, I sang.

And I'm thinking, poet friend,
  How you have, oftentimes,
Admired with pure unselfishness
  Those simple, homely rhymes.

For 'tis the genius of the soul
  (Though underneath a skin
Of dusky hue its fire may burn)
  Your unfeigned praises win.

Oh, that earth had more of beings
  With generous minds like yours,
Who alike, true worth and honor
  To the black and white secures.

'Accept, dear poet, then, my thanks
  For your glowing words of praise,
For the simple, homely, faulty rhymes
  Of my early girlhood days.

JASPER AT FORT MOULTRIE.

June 28, 1776.

"I'm only a sergeant!" Jasper said,
 "Not fit to go ahead
In the company of officers;
 I'm only a sergeant!" he said,

When to him a commission was offered,
 Giving lieutenant's rank
For the deed of bravery he had done,—
 Not 'mid bayonet's clash and clank,

But 'mid a terrific shower of shot
 And shell from the enemy's side;
He leaped o'er the bulwark and back again
 And our flag securely tied

To a sponge staff that was lying near,
 And hoisted it again
Courageously and bravely
 In the self-same place it had been,

Ere from its lofty position,
 Shattered by shot and shell,
Over the fort impregnable
 Of palmetto logs it fell.

All honor to you, brave Jasper!
　　We love and cherish your name
For your act of patriotism
　　Which was not done for fame;

But just for love of your country,
　　With patriotism true,
You braved your life for her colors,—
　　All honor and praise to you!

IN MEMORY OF WILLIAM HUGHES.

MY FRIEND AND CLASS-MATE.

It was in the month of June,
And the woods were all atune;
All atune with bird-music sweet and rare;
And the flowers were all in bloom,
Shedding forth their rich perfume
On the breezy atmosphere everywhere,

When from "Normal Hill" were we
And its cloister-life let free,
Not a bit of sadness then our hearts did fill;
For with the soft, filmy haze
Of September's shortening days
We hoped to meet again on "Normal Hill."

As adown the road we walked,
With free gayety we talked
Of blissful pleasures that would soon be ours,
Of picnics with dinners good,
Of wild rambles in the wood,
And of boatrides in the calm of evening hours.

I'm on "Normal Hill" to-day;
But, dear friend, you're still away.
I have ceased to hope to see you any more;
Till we meet in that high school
Where our Lord Himself shall rule,
Up in heaven on that shining, golden shore.

Little thought I, friend of mine,
You'd be called so soon to shine
In that galaxy of diadems up there;
But it was our Father's will,
And He speaks to-day "Be still,"
To my sad and sorrow-stricken heart down here.

VESPER SONG.

In the forest shadows dim
The birds now sing an evening hymn
In tones so soft and clear and sweet;
Their sweet sublimity complete.

The crickets chirp low on the hill,
The sound of grinding at the mill
Has ceased, and in the twilight gray
The miller wends his homeward way.

Slowly, in geometric line,
O'er meadows come the lowing kine;
Soft and gentle zephyrs blow,
Along the roadside fire-flies glow.

HE LEADETH ME.

When cloudless and sunlit skies o'erspread
Their azure robes above my head,
    When 'bout my pathway flowers grow
Richer than the Orient's blooms,
Than the Orient's sweet perfumes:
    'Tis pleasant then His will to know.

When winds are still and when the air
Is filled with music sweet and rare,
    Far sweeter than the sirens knew
Far sweeter strains than ever came
From Orpheus' harp wild beasts to tame:
    'Tis pleasant then His will to do.

But, oh, when dark and threat'ning clouds
My once fair sunlit sky enshrouds,
    And when bright flowers I do not see,
When winds like maddened billows roar,
When music charms my ears no more,—
    You ask how it's then with me?

How is it then my pathway's strewn
With sharpened stone and prickly thorn,
    Darkness about me, daylight gone?
It all I cannot understand,
But with my hand in His own hand
    I say: "Dear Father, lead me on."

KATHERINE.

To-day I am thinking of thee,
  Katherine,
And of the days that used to be,
  Katherine;
When together we two stood
In a quiet, leafy wood
By a little sylvan brook,
While we read each other's love as a book!

Ah! those days have long since flown,
  Katherine,
They are gone, forever gone,
  Katherine;
Those were days of "auld lang syne,"
Then I was yours and you were mine;
Through elysian fields we walked,
And of love we freely talked.

Yes, we loved each then,
  Katherine,
Life was then a sweet refrain,
  Katherine;
But I'm sad to-day, my dearie,
And the world seems, oh, so dreary,
For I see no more your face,
Feel no more your fond embrace.

THE END.

Rhymes from the Cumberland

By Effie Waller

Broadway Publishing Company
835 Broadway, New York

DEDICATION

I bring this little book
  Of simple rhymes, and few
With love sincere and pure
  To dedicate to you;
You whom I know and love,
  You who are my friends
And live among the mountains—
  The dear old Cumberlands.

—THE AUTHOR.

CONTENTS.

TO THE CUMBERLAND MOUNTAINS.

O Cumberland! O Cumberland!
 My own, my native hills,
For you, my dear old Cumberland
 With love my bosom thrills.

Your ridged and towering cliffs,
 What a beauty, what a wonder!
Which have withstood for centuries
 The lightning's flash and thunder.

Summer finds your craggy peaks
 No caps of whiteness wearing,
From base to crest you greet the eye
 With green majestic bearing.

In childhood's days upon your slopes
 How oft my feet have wandered,
How oft o'er your sublimity
 My childish mind has pondered.

With joy I've plucked the flowers that
  bloomed
 Within your dells and dales;
With eagerness I've watched the streams
 Plash through your wooded vales.

And I have seen within your vales

The timid cowering dove,
I've seen the eagle wing his flight
  Your lofty heights above.

But not solely for your beauty,
  Nor because my home is here,
Not for these alone, dear mountains
  In my heart I love you dear.

For within your soil lies buried
  'Neath the spruce pines and the flow'rs
The only love of my lost youth,
  Of my childhood's happy hours.

AMONG THE "BREAKS" OF BIG SANDY RIVER.

OCTOBER 1902.

The "Breaks" are a picturesque gorge about
five miles long in the Cumberland Mountains,
through which the beautiful Sandy river flows.

One halcyon day in Autumn
  Upon a wave-washed stone
I sat beside the river's edge,
  Musing, and all alone.

On either side of the river rose
  High towering towards the sky
The rugged, rock bound hills whereon
  I heard the spruce pines sigh.

The pipe reeds withered, brown and sere,
  The partridge, mellow drumming,
The many colored flying leaves
  Foretold of Winter's coming.

Above me calm and still there stretch'd
  A lovely lakelet blue,
Upon its shallow water swam
  Wild ducks of somber hue.

The gaudy crested pheasant bird
  Made low a whirring sound;
I heard a cataract that fell
  On boulders huge and round.

I watched the white and billowy clouds
  That floated lazily
With sun encircled edges through
  The purple tinted sky.

I never knew a sweeter look
  Of Nature ever wearing,
I never saw her more sublime,
  With more grand awesome bearing

Than when among Big Sandy's "Breaks"
  October last upon
That long-to-be-remembered day
  I spent with her alone.

My soul was thrilled with rhapsodies
  And filled with thoughts I can't express
O'er her grandeur, sublimity,
  And her simple loveliness.

Methought as on that stone I sat
  In wandering reverie,
"Were I a hermit, sure this place
  My hermitage would be."

EVENING AMONG THE CUMBER-
LANDS.

Among the rocky Cumberland
  A summer day is ending;
The woodman now with ax on arm
  His homeward way is wending.

The sun is hid from sight, but leaves
  A pleasant afterglow
On western, and quietude
  And peace are reigning now.

And from the woodland pasture
  The cattle slowly roam;
I hear the jingle of their bells
  Now on their journey home.

The robin gay has caroled
  His sweet and goodnight lay
And with his mate has gone to sleep
  Until another day.

The whippo'will so plaintive
  His night song has begun,
And everywhere's the music
  Of insects' ceaseless hum.

And now and then the night-hawk
　　With scream so loud and shrill,
I hear on some high distant peak
　　When all things else are still.

So calmly and so peacefully,
　　Just in this charmful way,
Among the rocky Cumberlands
　　Closes a summer day.

AT POOL POINT.

Pool Point is where the Cumberland
　　Causes an awkward bend
In Sandy river as it does
　　Its northward journey wend.

'Tis called Pool Point because there lies
　　Just at its base a pool
Made by the Sandy river; and
　　It sure is beautiful.

This spreading pool is almost round;
　　And it is always cool;
Its bosom almost waveless is;
　　Its depth is wonderful.

Is Pool Point rocky? I should say!
　　'Tis almost wholly rock,
Save a bit of clayey soil where grows
　　A growth of scrawny oak.

Once on this rocky point I stood

My sun-hat on my head
And threw a stone into its depths
    To watch the circles spread.

The sound was echoed from the hills,
    Then slowly died away;
The circles vanished one by one
    And left no trace where they

Had been a little while before:
    Still mused I standing on
That rugged, overhanging ledge
    Of rudely pictured stone.

"How easy it would be" I mused
    "To follow where I threw
That tiny stone and peacef'ly sleep
    Hidden away from view.

And would my friends forget me
    When there awhile I've lain?
Ah, yes, for Time's a balm for grief,
    For sorrow and for pain."

I turned my back towards the pool,
    And walked with rapid pace
Across the stony, woodland path
    Back to my boarding place.

"Forgive me, Father," thus I prayed,
    "Forgive thy erring child,
Who looking at thy handiwork
    Among these mountains wild;

"Who gazing at yon deep, wide pool
 Of waveless water mild
Should suicidal thoughts conceive.
 Forgive, forgive thy child."

THE LAKE ON THE MOUNTAIN.

The eastern sky of azure hue
 With colors bright were blended
As we with quick and buoyant steps
 The Cumberland ascended.

The air was breezy, fresh and warm;
 The morning was sublime;
The ground was strewn with colored leaves—
 For it was autumn time.

We stopped and plucked some wintergreen
 We gathered pine cones brown,
We paused awhile where chestnut trees
 Had dropped their harvest down.

So pleasantly we'd passed the time
 While climbing up the slope
We hardly realized it when
 We reached the mountain's top.

Suddenly a beauteous lake
 Our wondering entranced;
Upon its wave blown bosom
 The morning sunbeams danced.

Half hidden by the reeds and ferns

That yet were bright and green
Bathing quite near the water's edge
    Wild ducks by us were seen.

And clearly mirrored in the lake
    With leaves of varied hue
Were the trees that stood upon its shore
    'Neath heaven's dome of blue.

We sat upon a spruce pine's trunk
    That had uprooted been
By wind and storm and angled in
    The lake still and serene.

We homeward went ere evening came,
    But nothing did we take
With us except a string of fish
    From out the mountain lake.

ON BIG SANDY RIVER.

The sun-bathed hills were beautiful,
    The day was rich and fair
The wind was blowing fresh and cool,
    The atmosphere was rare.

When merry and light hearted in
    A "Jack-boat" painted red
Seeking some far off woodland scene
    We up the Sandy sped.

Far up the rippling, winding stream
    We found a pleasant spot,

'Twas beautiful in the extreme—
  Hid from the sunbeams hot.

The branches of the sycamore
  With spreading branches wide
Made a lovely archway o'er
  The river from each side.

We pushed our boat toward the shore
  And caref'ly tied her to
A drooping branch of sycamore
  Which near the water grew.

Along the shady, sandy bank
  Where grew the peppermint
Among the willows tall and rank
  We left our deep feet's print.

On a large rock smooth and bare
  We stopped awhile; and ate
A most delicious dinner there
  Which we'll not soon forget.

When shadows of the evening showed
  Upon the mountain green
Our painted boat we lightly rowed
  Adown the rippling stream.

With happy minds we homeward went
  Thinking we would never
Forget the pleasant day we'd spent
  On dear old Sandy River.

ELKHORN CITY.

O Elkhorn City, little town!
On which the Cumberland look down
    Fond and protectingly.
Around your northern border grows
The spruce pines, and the Sandy flows
    Among them tranquilly.

Your streets are ornamented well
With trees and cottages where dwell
    Ever contentedly
A people, hospitable and kind,
To Life and Duty never blind
    High minded proud and free.

O Elkhorn City! In my heart
I hold for you a goodly part
    Of love's devotion true;
And this my wish: That He above
May ever spread his wings of love
    Around and over you.

O SPRUCE PINES ON THE CUMBER-LANDS.

O spruce pines on the Cumberlands
    So stately and so tall,
So very grand and beautiful,
    Days gone by you recall.

Days of my childhood, happy days

When often I have played
Upon the slopes of these dear hills
　Within the spruce pines' shade.

He played with me—my sweetheart—then
　Under these spruce pines tall;
Of all the days that I have lived
　Those were happiest of all.

But one spring day upon these hills
　While zephyrs softly blew,
I stood beside my sweetheart's grave
　Strewed o'er with violets blue.

Among the spruce pines 'bove my head
　The birds sang sweet and clear
But the sweetness of their melody
　My sad heart could not cheer.

A score of years have passed since then,
　And still the spruce pines stand
Moaning a requiem for my dead
　Upon the Cumberland.

BEAUTIES OF THE CUMBERLAND.

He is not destitute of lore,—
　Far, far from it is he,—
Who doth the Cumberland adore,
　And love them reverently.

Methinks they who make their abode
　On plain and valley wide

Are not so near to heaven and God
   As those who here abide.

Among the dear old Cumberland
   How sweet is life to me,
Here beauties grow and e'er expand
   Each day for me to see.

Far from the city's strife and care
   I live a life obscure;
I breathe the sweet health-giving air
   And drink the water pure.

The rugged, rocky peaks I climb,
   Which bold and peerless stand,
Majestic, mighty, huge, sublime,
   So beautiful and so grand!

The wondrous works of God I view
   In every dell and nook;
And daily learn some lesson new
   From Nature's open book.

Here calm and wooded glens afford
   The noblest, purest kind
Of inspiration for the bard's
   Dreamy and gifted mind.

And here is music continually,
   Not tiresome, weird or dull;
And here are scenes for the artist's eye
   Lovely and beautiful.

How oft their grandeur I've admired

As 'neath them I have stood;
And it was they that me inspired
To love the pure and good.

How sweet among their vales to roam
And view their summits high;
Here may I ever have a home,
Here may I live and die!

ON DUTY'S KNOB.

The flush of a beautiful sunrise
Had gently melted away
And left no trace in the eastern sky
One morning early in May.

When with tiresome steps we'd climbed the
    slope
Of yon distant mountain high,
And were standing on its sunkissed top
'Neath a purple tinted sky.

With joy we listened to the birds
As we drank the sunshine in.
Far away we saw the town, but heard
We not its noise and din.

Breathed we the invigorating air
As beneath a copious shade
We sat and plucked the flowers fair
Which we into bouquets made.

With fragrance sweet they were scented
  Some were purple, some were gay.
But fairer than those flowers which
  We plucked and then threw away,

Was your own lovely expressive face
  Which anon was pensive then gay.
To me it had every womanly grace
  As I looked at it that day.

COURTSHIP AMONG THE CUMBER-LANDS.

Up from the woodland pasture
  Came farmer Thomson's son,
Driving his cattle homeward
  At the setting of the sun.

The long, narrow, winding pathway
  Was shaded here and there,
By stately growing elm trees
  And fringed with flowers fair.

Down this narrow, winding pathway,
  In homespun cotton gown,
Came Gracie, the youngest daughter
  Of blacksmith William Brown.

Leisurely she tripped along,
  Her feet were brown and bare;
Over her shoulders fluttered
  Soft braids of auburn hair.

She knew she would meet young Thomson,
  Her lover on the way,
Driving his cows from the pasture
  His 'customed duty each day.

But now as she sees him she blushes
  And twitches her pretty head,
And nervously fingers her apron
  Of checkered white and red.

How his eyes beam with love-light as
  He cries "Hello! Sweetheart Grace!"
And throws his arms about her,
  And clasps her in fond embrace.

Onward, and down the pathway
  The cattle slowly pass,
Nibbling at blossomed daisies
  And bits of straggling grass,

The golden sun has sunk behind
  The mountains steep and tall;
And the moon is shining brightly,
  Twilight is over all.

Among the stately elm trees
  The night winds softly sigh—
And still the lovers linger
  Beneath the moonlit sky.

MY NATIVE MOUNTAINS.

I love my native mountains,
   The dear old Cumberland,
Rockribbed and everlasting,
   How great they are, and grand!

I love each skyward reaching peak,
   Each glassy glade and dale,
Each moss-and-fern-clad precipice
   Each lovely flower decked vale.

I love each vine-hung rocky glen
   I love each dark ravine
Though there may hide the catamount
   And wild dog sly and mean.

I love my mountains' forests
   Varied and beautiful
I love her springs and waterfalls,
   So pure and wonderful.

I love her richly plumaged birds
   The pheasant and the jay,
The merry scarlet tanager,
   The woodpeck bright and gay.

How oft among these mountains
   Has the silvery music clear
From the lark's throat cheered the traveler,
   And the honest mountaineer.

But more than these old mountains

Which with wonder I revere
I love with true devotion
   The people who live here.

So here's with love sincere and dear
   For her sons of brawn and worth;
And her daughters pure and lovely,
   The fairest types of earth.

TO A SPRING IN THE CUMBERLANDS.

Gurgling spring in sylvan beauty
   Almost hid away from view;
From your own bright sparkling water
   I will drink a health to you.

Beach and oak tree reaching skyward
   Guard you from the sunlight's heat;
And from this overhanging stone
   Comes a breath of flowers sweet.

In your water clear and cold
   Warbling birds their plumage lave;
From your brink o'ergrown with mosses
   Dainty fern fronds gently wave.

Huntmen here have often lingered
   Drinking of your water clear;
And you've often quenched the thirst
   Of the agile, antlered deer.

So here's a health dear sparkling spring
   Gurgling from the mountain's side,

With a wish that in your beauty
  You will ever here abide.

Oct. 4, 1902.

SUNRISE ON THE CUMBERLANDS.

    The Chimney Rocks are huge chimney shaped rocks from which a vapor resembling smoke continually rises.

We sat upon the Chimney Rocks
  O'ergrown with lichens gray,
Waiting for the sunlight warm
  To clear the mist away.

The Chimney Rocks crown a peak
  Of Cumberland mountain which
O'erlooks the Sandy river
  In picturesqueness rich.

Skyward in rugged bold relief
  Without a bush or tree
To make their prominence less marked
  They tower in majesty.

Wet were our garments with the dew,
  Tired were our feet and sore;
For we had climbed a good long mile
  Of stony path before

We reached those rocks whereon our guide
  Time and again had been

With others ere us to see the sun
   His daily course begin.

He (our guide) had said to us
   In rustic language: "You
Of sunrise from the Chimney Rocks
   Will get a lovely view."

I would that you had been with us
   On dear old Cumberland;
Have sat with us upon those rocks
   And have seen that sunrise grand.

The sunbeams kissed the mountain tops;
   The mist was cleared away;
The eastern sky was streaked and splatched
   With colors bright and gay.

While we bared our heads to gaze
   On distant suntipped peaks
The scented morning zephyrs fanned
   Our hot and flushing cheeks.

And, I doubt not the self same thoughts
   Were pondered in each mind,
As we looked down the rocky slope
   Which we had lately climbed

With toilsome steps to reach those rocks
   Where we could see the sun
Appear in glorious splendor
   Above the horizon.

Though toilsome was the walk it seemed

As nothing since our eyes
With pleasant joy had feasted on
That glorious sunrise.

Sometimes the pathway which He bids
Us walk in here below
Is often stony, and ofttimes
Beside it thistles grow.

Sometimes the misty clouds o'er hang
Our stony pathway hard;
Sometimes we almost starve for rest
We get so *very* tired!

But then above the gloomy clouds
There's sunshine, and we know
We'll reach a place not strewn with stones
Where thistles do not grow.

And when we reach that upper land
So bright, so pure and fair
Forgotten will the hardships be
We had in getting there.

SUNSET ON THE CUMBERLAND.

Upon the "Chimneys" yesterday
We sat beneath the trees
While sang the birds and softly blew
The flower scented breeze.

You should have been with us upon
Those "Chimney Rocks" and seen

The golden sun in grandeur sink
  Behind the hill-tops green.

Like bars across the western sky
  Such gorgeous streaks of red,
Such brilliant hues of yellow
  Of blue and pink were spread.

So richly blended were those hues
  They cast a lovely splendor
Which words cannot describe upon
  The budding tree tops tender.

Had Rembrandt been with us I doubt
  Quite much if he on canvas
Could have portrayed with brush and paint
  That sunset's loveliness.

Long sat we on those moss grown rocks
  With eyes and minds untiring,
The beauty and the grandeur of
  That sunset scene admiring.

A MOUNTAIN PICTURE

We sat within the cabin old,
  'Twas built of logs, and small;
The blazing fire of beechen sticks
  Lit up the dingy wall.

Discerned we with our searching eyes
  While glowed the fire's bright light,
On strong supports above the door
  A rifle polished bright.

The crickets chirped solemnly
  Among the chimney's clay,
Dozing upon the hearthstone wide
  A brindled kitten lay.

We chatted with our host who had
  For more than three score year,
Lived among the Cumberlands
  A sturdy mountaineer.

He sat with legs crossed, loosely clad
  In home spun suit of grey,
While smoke in billowy waves of blue
  Curled from his pipe of clay.

He was our guide while we were there
  Among those mountains high;
Whose every rill and valley were
  Familiar to his eye.

He told of when ferocious beasts
  Roamed o'er those mountains wild;
He told us of the time when he
  An Indian chief had killed.

Yes, many tales he told to us
  Of ancient deeds performed
By him among the Cumberlands
  With knife and musket armed.

And while we listened to those tales
  More fanciful than truthful,
We noted well our host's blue eyes
  Large, sparkling, keen, and youthful.

The tranquil peace and happiness
   That sweet contentment brings,
And which our host possessed is not
   A heritage for kings.

Nor for those who daily walk
   The crowded ways of life,
Eager for gain and eminence
   Though won and held through strife.

'Twas thus I pondered long that night
   In meditation deep,
While lying on my bed before
   I closed my eyes in sleep.

I coveted my host who lived
   With peace of mind unbounded,
Beside the Sandy river
   By mountain walls surrounded.

PART II

CONTENTS

THERE'S BEAUTY ALL AROUND US.

All around us there is beauty
    On the leaves of Nature's book,
And while in the path of duty
    Ought we not at them to look?

Oh, why should we within a field
    Of fresh blooming roses rare
See but the thorns that're half-concealed
    Underneath the blossoms fair?

Or why should we the lilies tread
    With our clumsy, careless feet?
"Consider them," Our Savior said,
    "In their loveliness complete."

While daily through the world we move
    With duty's path around us,
Let's train our eyes to see and love
    The beauties that surround us.

Let us sometimes watch the sun rise
    As the moments hasten by,
Glowing with rich resplendent dyes
    In the far off eastern sky.

And at morning let us listen

While the birds their carols sing,
While the silvery dew-drops glisten
And the cow-bells faintly ring.

When beneath the elm we rest
While blows the evening wind
As the Day-god in the west
Sinks the mountain's crest behind.

When the stars are faintly peeping
From the heavens one by one,
When shadows are dimly creeping,
When the busy day is done.

Then as we meditate and dream
With Nature wonderingly,
Perhaps our cares will lighter seem,
And our work less irksome be.

VIOLETS.

Oh, lovely, lovely violets,
So dainty and so blue,
So modest yet so beautiful,
Whene'er I look at you

I mind me of a gone-by day,
When in a woodland glade,
Beside a purling brooklet,
Beneath an elm's shade.

We sat and plucked the violets
That blossomed by us there,

Shedding their sweet perfume
  Upon the woodland air.

We made sweet nose-gays of their blooms,
  We tried our fortunes, too,
With them, though long ago that's been,
  They told our fortunes true.

THE MAPLE'S LEAVES WERE SCARLET.

The maple's leaves were scarlet,
  The golden rods were bright,
The birdies to the South land
  Had winged their homeward flight.

The katydids were calling
  Beneath the spreading yew,
In hollows near the forest's edge
  The grapes were turning blue.

The sumac's crimson berries shone
  By brook and dusty road,
Within our dooryards gorgeous blooms
  Of tall chrysanth'mums glowed.

When hand in hand they vowed to walk
  Life's pathway here together,
Through poverty or riches and
  Through fair or stormy weather.

And share together all the pains
  And pleasures that await them,
Through health or sickness love none else
  'Till death should separate them.

BEAUTIFUL MOON.

Beautiful goddess of the night,
  Shining gently from above,
Whisper to me, oh, moon so bright,
  Whisper of my absent love.
Moon, oh, beautiful moon, so bright,
Shedding gently your radiant light,
Tell me to-night, fair moon, won't you,
Does my sweetheart love me true?

Moon, as upon my pillow white
  Your bright beams fall from above,
Bathing my head with mellow light,
  Oh, let me dream of my love.
Moon, oh, beautiful moon, so bright,
Let me dream of my love to-night;
Tell me of him, oh, fair moon, do,
Tell me does he love me true?

A MEADOW BROOK.

There's a quiet nook by a meadow brook
  In my old Kentucky home far away,
'Tis a cool retreat from the scorching heat
  How I wish I were there to-day.

There to lie on the grass while the breezes pass,
  Where the violet sweetly grows,
And high overhead the elm trees spread
  Their vine and leaf-clad boughs.

'Tis indeed a treat supremely sweet
  For the nature-loving soul;

There lilies wave and gently lave
  In the water clear and cool.

How often there from perplexing care
  Listening to the brooklet's flow,
Have I laid at rest on the grassy breast
  Of Mother Earth long ago.

Those days have sped, have swiftly fled
  On the wings of time away,
But in memory yet I can't forget
  That meadow brook far away.

ON RECEIVING A DEER-SKIN.

TO W. K.

With my bare feet on my deer-skin,
  The firelight glowing bright,
In my old and creaky rocker
  I sit alone to-night.

While imagination holds me
  Within her fond embrace,
With the lithe, fleet-footed deer
  I rove from place to place.

Far out among the western wilds,
  Beyond the turbid tide
Of the Mississippi river,
  Beyond prairies wide.

I gaze upon the geysers high,
  And boiling springs of water,

I see the great Missouri where
   Enormous cedars border.

I see the Indian's bark canoe
   Adown its bosom dashing,
I see majestic cataracts
   And hear their mighty splashing.

I see the panther and the wolf,
   And birds with plumage rare,
I see the horned buffalo,
   And shaggy, grizzly bear.

I wander through dark fastnesses
   Where weird breezes blow,
I climb the craggy rugged peaks
   Cered o'er with ice and snow.

Among the Rockies' vales I pluck
   The brightest beauties strewn
By Flora's lavish hand, and find
   Rare specimens of stone.

I thank you for this deer-skin rug
   Before my fireside bright,
And my imaginative journey
   To the western wilds to-night.

WHEN YOU ARE WITH ME.

Richer tints the western sky
   Shows at sunset, darling mine,
Which all artist's paints defy:

Gorgeous, splendid, e'en divine,
  When you are with me.

And when the lowliest flower
  In Spring its leaves unfold,
(Be its home on hill or moor)
  Sweeter fragrance seems to hold,
    When you are with me.

Where flows yon winding stream
  Among the alders green,
More lovely does its waters seem,
  More calm and more serene,
    When you are with me.

In grove and meadow sing the birds
  More sweetly and more gayly,
When I'm listening to your hopeful words
  Of our futurity,
    When you are with me.

A RECOLLECTION.

Once there in my garden fair
Sang a bird of plumage rare,
From its throat there came to greet
My ear sweet music—strangely sweet.

Once a flower of lovely hue
In this self same garden grew,
Blossomed—oh, so sweetly there
That its breath perfumed the air.

Once a flower of lovely hue
This same garden murmured through,
Over shining stones it played,
Softest, richest music made.

In this garden 'neath a tree
That cast its copious shade for me,
Was a restful cool retreat
From the noonday's scorching heat.

Now no richly plumaged bird
Singing in my garden's heard,
A milder zone it's sought than this;
Ah, its sweet songs how I miss.

Now no flower of lovely hue
Glittering with morning dew
Sheds its perfume in the air—
It has dropped its petals fair.

In my garden near the hill
Flows the self same brooklet still,
But it makes no rippling sound
For with ice and snow 'tis bound.

And the elm tree that made
Such a copious, cooling shade,
Void of foliage is it now,
Naked each brown spreading bough.

Birdie, flower, brooklet, tree,
You all now are gone from me;
But 'till now I never knew
That I loved you as I do.

Little thought I, dear sweetheart,
On that morn ere we did part
When from me you claimed a kiss
That your presence I would miss;
For ere then I did not know—
Did not dream I loved you so.

Could we only know before
'Tis too late what is in store
For us; what of storm and rain,
What of sadness, grief and pain.

We'd enjoy the glad sunlight
While it lasts ere comes the night,
And our friends so kind and dear
We would love and prize and cheer.

IN THE YEARS THAT ARE TO COME.

When my hair is thin and gray,
   When there's wrinkles on my brow;
When my eyes are dim, and when
   Feeble is my step and slow,
This one question I would ask,
   This one question, sweetheart, dear,
Will you love me then as now,
   Love me truly and sincere.

"THE BEST OF ALL, GOD IS WITH US."

DYING WORDS OF JOHN WESLEY.

When trials hard and sore we meet,
When thorns are piercing our tired feet,

When heavy clouds o'erspread the sky,
When winds are wild and waves dash high,
　　"The best of all, God is with us."

When earthly friends unfaithful prove,
When kindred hearts have ceased to love,
When grief the heart has sorely tried,
When Satan tempts on every side,
　　"The best of all, God is with us."

When we pass through death's valley dark
Of earthly light, without a spark,
When earthly friends from us have gone,
When earthly help and hopes have flown,
　　"The best of all, God is with us."

And when we reach that shining shore
Up yonder, where we die no more,
Up yonder, where from sin we're free,
The sweetest fact to us will be,
　　"The best of all, God is with us."

THERE'S A BRIGHT AND BEAUTIFUL CITY.

There's a bright and beautiful city,
　A beautiful city on high;
A beautiful city for you and me,
　Far, far beyond the sky.

The streets of that city with gold are paved,
　The gates are of pearls pure and white,
And the walls are of rare and precious stones
　Most beautiful and bright.

In that city are never-fading flowers,
  There the tree of Life ever grows;
And the river of Life so clear and pure
  Through that beautiful city flows.

No moon nor stars ever shine there
  For there never is any night,
Nor no sun is there to shine by day
  For the Savior is the light.

The inhabitants never do get sick
  In that fair city on high,
And they never need any graveyards there
  For they never, never die.

HE IS RISEN.

"He is not here," the angel said
To Mary, who, with silent tread,
With weeping eyes and bowed down head,
Sought her Lord among the dead.

"The tomb is empty, come and see;
Your Lord's not here, oh, no, not He;
This is His tomb, and these His clothes,
But He's not here, for He has rose."

May we like Him—our Savior rise
From things of low and weak disguise,
Rise from the trifling things of earth
To things of high intrinsic worth.

Rise from the world's perplexing strife

Unto a higher, nobler life;
A life from sin's pollution free,
A life of spotless purity!

TO AN OLD CLASS-MATE.

As your letter I read, dear Mary,
    To-night in my room alone,
I am made happy, very,
    As I think of days by gone.

Now at your face, my dearie,
    With fanciful eyes I gaze,
And hear again your voice so cheery
    As in the olden days.

Those days of our school career
    When life was full of glee,
Although I was your senior, dear,
    You seemed a mother to me.

O'er books with pensive eyes we'd gaze
    To solve the problems there,
Which fitted us for life's broad ways
    And possibilities, my dear.

We walk life's broadened ways to-day,
    Solve at its problems, too,
More deep and more perplexing they
    Than those our text-books knew.

Since you were with me, Mary, dear,
    The years have sped away, how fast;

Some spent in smiles and some in tears,
  However spent they're of the past.

DO YOU KNOW?

Do you know the grapes are purpling,
  And the nuts are falling down?
Do you know the leaves are turning,
  Turning yellow, red and brown?

Do you know the grass has withered,
  That it does no longer grow?
Do you know the white field-daisy
  Faded, faded long ago?

Do you know that in the orchard
  Apple trees are bending down
With their weight of red, red pippins
  And of russets golden brown?

Do you know down by the roadside
  By the road you oft have trod,
Blooming lovely 'spite of dust
  Is the gaudy golden rod?

Do you know that in the cornfield
  Heaps of yellow pumpkins lie?
Do you know that to the Southland
  Birdies have begun to fly?

If you'd leave the smoky city
  You would know these things, my dear,
And would only look about you,
  You would know that Autumn's here.

I NEED THEE EVERY HOUR.

"I need Thee every hour,
  Most gracious Lord,"
With majesty and power
  With one accord.

Sang the village choir at church
  Truthful words of prayer,
Could we but know how much
  We need Thee here.

How much we need Thy guidance
  When roads are drear,
How much we need Thy aidance
  When sin is near.

Believing on Thy precious word
  And mercy free,
May I thus ever pray, "Dear Lord,
  I need, oh, I need Thee."

"HOW BEAUTIFUL IT IS TO BE WITH GOD."

DYING WORDS OF FRANCES E. WILLARD.

"How beautiful it is to be with God."
Truer and sweeter words by dying lips
  Than those above were never said,
Courage and hope and comfort, all, they brought
  To those who mourned around your bed.

"How beautiful it is to be with God."
For many years you realized this fact
　　Walking beside Him day by day
With unfeigned love along life's checkered way,
　　Having no other wish but to obey.

"How beautiful it is to be with God."
Like you endeavoring hard to 'stablish right;
　　Helping seeds of kindness to sow,
Helping to cheer the lonely hearts, and bring
　　A ray of sunshine where you go.

"How beautiful it is to be with God."
Lovingly to sympathize with those
　　Whose lives are saddened and to speak
In mild and gentle tones reproving oft
　　Our brothers who are wayward and weak.

"How beautiful it is to be with God."
When life is closing fast and visions of
　　The mysterious future appear,
'Tis beautiful indeed amid the gloom
　　To feel, to know that He is near.

"How beautiful it is to be with God."
Dear soul, we hope, we feel assured that you
　　In bliss unbounded now behold
Your dear Redeemer face to face and walk
　　With Him the City's streets of gold.

SING A SONG OF AUTUMN.

Sing a song of Autumn,
　　Flowers no more in bloom,

Shedding all around us
　　Their balmy, rich perfume.

In vain we look for flowers,
　　For they're faded all, and dead,
But the woodland still is brilliant
　　With bright-hued leaves instead.

The frost has nipped the clover
　　And left the meadows brown;
Hickory nuts and chestnuts
　　From the trees are falling down.

CHRISTMAS.

In a country far, far away,
　　Far beyond the rolling sea,
To the little town of Bethle'em
　　Shepherds wond'ring came to see
Him of whom the heavenly choir
　　Sang with gladness, sang with might,
Of His birth and of His glory
　　On that holy sacred night.

Loud those Judean hills re-echoed,
　　Loud and joyously they rang,
What the angel choir so sweetly
　　And so gladly, gladly sang.
Sang they of the Father's mercy
　　Who to us the Christ-babe gave
For our own and full redemption,
　　Mercy rich and free to save!

It is not ours to listen now

To a host of angels sing
Loud and sweet the welcome tidings
    Which to earth they gladly bring,
Nor ours with wonderment to gaze
    O'er a manger cradle low,
As did once those pious shepherds
    In Judea long ago.

For the Redeemer that was born
    In that country far away,
His coming has not been forgot,
    Still He lives and reigns to-day.
Oh, holy one of Bethlehem,
    Come be born in us to-day,
"Love divine, all love excelling,"
    In our hearts hold perfect sway.

ON RECEIVING A SOUVENIR POST-CARD.

On the little desk before me
    A pictured post-card lies,
Fondly I'm looking at it
    With saddened tear-dimmed eyes.

The postman came this morning
    And brought this card to me,
It was sent from Kentucky, where
    My childhood's home used to be.

The rustic scene in black and white,
    Imperfect tho' and small,
Engraved upon this post-card,
    Might not interest you at all.

You may not care to look at it,
  What matter if you don't;
Your not having any interest, for
  This pictured post-card won't.

Make less for me the memories
  And thoughts of "ye olden tyme,"
Freighted with love and tenderness
  And which to-day entwine.

Fondly around my yearning heart
  As with tear-dimmed eyes I gaze
At this bit of scenery and think
  Over my childhood days.

I think of one in particular
  Who has figured so much in my life,
One to whom I was playmate in childhood
  Afterward sweetheart and wife.

There's the winding Sandy river
  And the "Big Rocks" by its side,
Where together we've sat fishing,
  Or looking across the tide.

Have wondered at the steamboats
  Painted in colors gay
On the other side of the river
  Smoking and puffing away.

Or at the town in the distant
  Sometimes we'd sit and gaze
And dream bright dreams of the future—
  Air castles of childhood days.

And if our thoughts and opinions
   On matters would differ then,
We'd fall out and quarrel, but always
   Would forgive and make up again.

There's the "forks" in the old country road
   Shaded with sycamores cool,
Where each afternoon we parted
   On our way home from school.

And he, always courteous and gallant
   With manly pride and grace,
Would carry my books and lunch pail
   To this our parting place.

Those days are gone, forever gone,
   Those care-free days of childhood,
Yet, I would not call them back to live
   Over again if I could.

For he, my childhood's playmate,
   My girlhood's lover and chum,
Still walks life's pathway with me
   And for many years we've come

Sometimes through darkened valleys,
   Sometimes on the mountain's height,
Sometimes 'neath cloud-hung heavens,
   Sometimes in the sunshine bright.

We are closely united now,
   For we're married and we feel
Each other's interests more keenly
   And we're chums and lovers still.

THE 'FRISCO EARTHQUAKE.

While the earth shook and trembled and hungry
    flames wild
Leaped skyward as building on building were
    piled.
They perish by thousands, fathers and mothers,
Husbands, wives, sisters, sweethearts and broth-
    ers;
The rich and the poor, the high and the low,
In the beautiful city of San Francisco.
Sad, sad was their fate; sad, sad was their fate
In the fair city of the Golden Gate;
In the city of flowers and sunlight,
In the city so gay and so bright,
Sad, ah, sad was their fate!

Death came when the first rosy tints of the
    morn
In the eastern sky were beginning to dawn.
What hopes and ambitions were then holding
    sway
In the hearts of those people on San 'Frisco bay
When death came to claim them eternity knows,
Eternity knows and can only disclose.
Sad, sad was their fate; sad, sad was their fate
In the fair city of the Golden Gate;
In the city of flowers and sunlight,
In the city so gay and so bright,
Sad, ah, sad was their fate!

THE "BACHELOR GIRL."

She's no "old maid," she's not afraid
   To let you know she's her own "boss,"
She's easy pleased, she's not diseased,
   She is not nervous, is not cross.

She's no desire whatever for
   Mrs. to precede her name,
The blessedness of singleness
   She all her life will proudly claim.

She does not sit around and knit
   On baby caps and mittens,
She does not play her time away
   With puggy dogs and kittens.

And if a mouse about the house
   She sees, she will not jump and scream;
Of handsome beaux and billet doux
   The "bachelor girl" does never dream.

She does not puff and frizz and fluff
   Her hair, nor squeeze and pad her form.
With painted face, affected grace,
   The "bachelor girl" ne'er seeks to charm.

She reads history, biography,
   Tales of adventure far and near,
On sea or land, but poetry and
   Love stories rarely interest her.

She's lots of wit, and uses it,
   Of "horse sense," too, she has a store;

The latest news she always knows,
  She scans the daily papers o'er.

Of politics and all the tricks
  And schemes that politicians use,
She knows full well and she can tell
  With eloquence of them her views.

An athlete that's hard to beat
  The "bachelor girl" surely is,
When playing games she makes good aims
  And always strictly minds her "biz."

Amid the hurry and the flurry
  Of this life she goes alone,
No matter where you may see her
  She seldom has a chaperon.

But when you meet her on the street
  At night she has a "32,"
And she can shoot you, bet your boots,
  When necessity demands her to.

Her heart is kind and you will find
  Her often scattering sunshine bright
Among the poor, and she is sure
  To always advocate the right.

On her *pater* and her *mater*
  For her support she does not lean,
She talks and writes of "Woman's Rights"
  In language forceful and clean.

She does not shirk, but does her work,

Amid the world's fast hustling whirl,
And come what may, she's here to stay,
The self-supporting "bachelor girl."

THERE'S A MOUND IN WEST VIRGINIA.

IN MEMORY OF WILLIAM C. PENN.
November 1905.

There's a mound in West Virginia,
    Which was made one year ago,
In November's chilly weather
    When the earth was wrapped in snow;
When the skies were dull and frowning,
    And the birds had flown away
To the warm and sunny South land,
    Save dear Robin-red-breast gay.

The dearest treasure which my heart
    On earth has ever found,
Sleeps undisturbed underneath
    That West Virginia mound.
They tell me 'tis a common thing
    To grieve for loved ones gone;
But ah, this fact makes not my grief
    More easy to be borne!

The hope that I again shall meet
    My dear lost friend somewhere,
In a far more lovely clime than this
    'Mid heavenly mansions fair,
Will not remove the sadness from
    My yearning spirit weak

Is not enough to keep away
   The tear-drops from my cheek.

SOME DAY.

The pathway thou art walking now
   With weary feet, dear one,
Hedged in by briers and poison vine,
   Bestrewn with sticks and stone:
Oh, grumble not, 'twill lead thee to
   A smoother and a better way
Shaded by broad-armed elm trees
   And fringed with flowers—some day.

Oh, weary toiling one,
   Whose brow is wet with sweat,
Mind not thy task, though it be,
   Mind not the scorching heat.
Toil on and sing a little bit
   In cheerful tones and gay
While at thy work, and don't forget
   There's rest for thee—some day.

And thou, bereaved one,
   Why grieve and sorrow on
With low-dropped head and weeping eyes
   For loved ones dead and gone.
Believe and trust the Father
   Who has taken them away,
Knoweth best and will give them
   Again to thee—some day.

Lines written on the fly-leaf of a volume of poems presented to Mary Elliot Flanery.

Dear Mrs. Flanery:
   As your eager eyes peruse
      These pages over and again,
   These verses sent me by the muse
      I'd have you know that not in vain,
   You wrote those sincere words of praise
      Of me who sprang from humble birth,
   Sprang from a race down trod and low,
      Cursed, abused, despised of earth.
   A pleasant fact it is to know
      (Though now it's not Anti-slavery days)
   That that same principle possessed
      By Sumner, Phillips, Whittier, Stowe
   Vibrates within your noble breast,
      Which fortune cannot overthrow,
   Which ridicule cannot remove.
      A heart more generous than your own
   To fredom and to human kind
      The flight of years have never known,
   Have never, never dared to find.
      Live long your principles to prove.